"Teamwork wins championships, and *Coaching Team* the secrets for success not only on the basketball co Anyone committed to being part of a team or buildii this book."

—Dwyane Wade
Miami Heat, NBA All-Star, 2006 NBA Finals MVP,
Marquette University, All-American

"Leadership, core values, team unity—we have found these elements to be of extreme importance in the building of successful teams. In this book, the authors describe in easy-to-read concepts how to use these same elements to lay a firm foundation for winning teams. This book will be an excellent resource for all coaches."

—Pat Summitt
Head Women's Basketball Coach,
University of Tennessee,
6-Time NCAA National Champions,
All-Time Wins Leader in NCAA Division I Basketball

"*Coaching Team Basketball* should be in every coach's library. In clear and specific fashion, Tom Crean and Ralph Pim discuss the importance of team dynamics and how to create a winning culture. Their examples from the game of basketball and the parallel lessons from military training are outstanding."

—Dean Lockwood, Assistant Basketball Coach,
University of Tennessee

"Tom Crean and Ralph Pim are outstanding educators. In their book *Coaching Team Basketball*, they do a great job of simplifying what it takes to work together as a unit. It is a great resource for coaches and players."

—Mike Brey, Head Basketball Coach,
University of Notre Dame

"This book is a must-read for all coaches. From my experiences as a high school, college, NBA, and European coach, I know that *Coaching Team Basketball* presents valuable lessons that can be applied to all levels of coaching. It's superbly written and provides an easy-to-follow blueprint for team success."

—Don Casey, Executive Vice-President, NBA Coaches Association,
Vice Chair of the President's Council
on Fitness and Sport (1994–2000)

"Tom and Ralph are two of the top team builders I know. I have watched Ralph build successful teams for 25 years and he is a person of the highest integrity. Tom is one of the coaching giants in the game today. In *Coaching Team Basketball*, they have identified the ingredients for unleashing the power of teamwork in any sport. Everyone should read it."

—Dave Collins, Coach, Colorado Rockies

"I wholeheartedly recommend *Coaching Team Basketball* for coaches at all levels who wish to build stronger teams. Tom and Ralph's winning system is a combination of detail, simplicity, and common sense. Together they provide the keys that will make a difference in your program. Don't miss it!"

—Bill Raftery, CBS Sports Broadcaster

"Tom Crean and Ralph Pim are two of the finest basketball minds and teachers of the game that I have had the privilege to know. This book skillfully provides their insights into the game, how it should be played, and how it should be taught. It is a must-read for every coach, player, or fan who wants a deeper appreciation of the finer points of basketball. Tom and Ralph never stop learning about the game and sharing what they learn. *Coaching Team Basketball* provides invaluable and thoughtful insight about basketball. There are a lot of years of incredible experience, thoughtful preparation, hard work, and great success between the covers of this book."

—Jay Bilas, ESPN Basketball Analyst

"Tom Crean and Ralph Pim are two of the best in basketball at teaching and building teams. Together they've provided an excellent blueprint for team building that basketball fans of all ages will benefit from. Watching the progress of the Marquette program during Tom's tenure confirms what I've always known, that his tireless work ethic, preparation, and instruction are why his teams are successful."

—Tom Izzo, Head Basketball Coach, Michigan State University, 2000 NCAA National Champions

"Tom Crean and Ralph Pim have written the perfect book on the power of teamwork. All coaches, at any level, who want to see their teams play up to or surpass their potential, must read this remarkable book."

—Morgan Wootten,
Naismith Basketball Hall off Fame, Class of 2000,
High School Coach of the Twentieth Century

COACHING TEAM BASKETBALL

Develop Winning Players with a Team-First Attitude

TOM CREAN AND **RALPH PIM**

New York Chicago San Francisco Lisbon London Madrid Mexico City
Milan New Delhi San Juan Seoul Singapore Sydney Toronto

Library of Congress Cataloging-in-Publication Data

Crean, Tom.
    Coaching team basketballl : develop winning players with a team-first attitude /
by Tom Crean and Ralph Pim.
        p.   cm.
    Includes index.
    ISBN 0-07-146565-0 (alk. paper)
    1. Basketball—Coaching.   I. Pim, Ralph L.   II. Title.

GV885.3.C74   2007
796.3307'7—dc22   2006020502

All photos are courtesy of Marquette University.

1 2 3 4 5 6 7 8 9 10 11 12 13 14 15 16 17 18 19   DOC/DOC   0 9 8 7 6

ISBN-13: 978-0-07-146565-6
ISBN-10:   0-07-146565-0

Interior design by Think Design, LLC

McGraw-Hill books are available at special quantity discounts to use as premiums and
sales promotions, or for use in corporate training programs. For more information, please
write to the Director of Special Sales, Professional Publishing, McGraw-Hill, Two Penn
Plaza, New York, NY 10121-2298. Or contact your local bookstore.

This book is printed on acid-free paper.

To my wife, Joani,
who is willing to run through fire for me and shares
my passion for life and the sport of basketball.
In addition to raising our three wonderful children,
no woman was ever more dedicated to the welfare of her husband
than Joani. She is my confidante and best friend,
who gracefully can be found just outside the limelight
where she prefers to be.

To my mother, Marjorie,
who demonstrated a strong love for my sister
and me as well as numerous foster children who needed
her love and guidance. Her resolve to allow me to pursue
my lifelong dreams is the major reason why I am coaching
major college basketball today.

To my loving sister, Michelle.
I have always strived to protect you from anyone or
anything that might hurt you and I always will. I will
always be there for you, as you have been for me.

To Jack, Jackie, Jim, John, and Miah Harbaugh.
You are the best in-laws and extended family that a person
could ever hope for. Thanks for everything you do!

TC

To my beautiful wife, Linda.
You have brought joy and happiness into my life.
Thanks for your understanding and patience through
many long days of writing. I love you with all my heart.

To all the officers that I have worked with at the
United States Military Academy. Thank you for your selfless
service to our nation. You are leaders of character
and a daily inspiration to me. Go Army!

RP

To all the players we have had the honor of coaching
at Alma, Michigan State, Western Kentucky, Pittsburgh,
Marquette, Northwestern Louisiana, Central Michigan,
William and Mary, Limestone, Barberton High School,
and Mount Pleasant High School.

TC AND RP

Contents

Foreword by Dwyane Wade   xi

Acknowledgments   xiii

Alma College: Where It All Began by Michael Broeker   xv

Key to Diagrams   xix

PART 1   Teamwork

1 Where Has the Team Play Gone?   3
       The New Generation   4
       The Decline of U.S. Men's Basketball   5
       Differences Between U.S. and Foreign Players   6
       The Influence of the NBA   7
       Where Does Basketball Go from Here?   8
       An Application Model for Team Play   9

2 Teamwork Trumps Individual Talent   11
       Miracle on Ice   12
       Dynasty of the 1990s   13
       The Model Franchise in the NFL   14
       Princeton: "The Little Engine That Could"   15
       There Is No "I" in Team   16
       One Team, One Fight   19
       Teamwork Must Be Taught   19
       Selfless Service   20
       A Team Wins and Loses Together   22

3 The Meaning of Team Play   25
       Qualities of a Team Player   26

Role Models for Team Play	31
Esprit de Corps	34
Coach's Game Plan	36

PART 2   Blueprint for Team Play

4	Lead from the Front	43
	Advice for Young Coaches	45
	Characteristics of an Effective Coach	46
	Value-Based Coaching	53
	Coach's Game Plan	54

5	Build Your Program on Core Values	57
	Define Your Core Values	59
	What Are the Core Values of Your Team?	67
	Keep Your Core Values at the Forefront	68
	Team Ownership of the Core Values	68
	Coach's Game Plan	72

6	Begin with the End in Mind	73
	Blue-Sky Thinking	74
	Shared Vision	75
	Put Your Vision in Writing	75
	The Power of Visual Images	77
	Coach's Game Plan	80

7	Select Talented Team Players	81
	Character	82
	Have Prospects Watch Practice	90
	Motor Skills	90
	What Do You Search for in Players?	93
	Selecting Assistant Coaches	94
	Coach's Game Plan	97

8	Promote Teamwork and Team Unity	99
	Team Ownership	100
	Define Roles	103

Line of Commitment   105
Buddy System   105
Shrink the Circle   106
Peer Coaching   108
Stretch the Talent of Your Players   108
Thought for the Day   111
Team Communication   112
Outside Speakers   116
Spotlighting   117
Coach's Game Plan   118

PART 3   Why Teams Win

9 Statistical Factors That Determine Winning
       and Losing   121
   1978 Research Study   122
   2005 Research Study   122
   Results   123
   Conclusions   126
   Implementation   127

10 Offensive Keys for Team Success   129
   Get to the Free Throw Line   130
   Pass the Ball Inside   131
   Offensive Rebounding   138
   See the Floor and Read the Defense   139
   Dribble Penetration   140
   Setting Screens   141
   Receiving Screens   142
   Screens-on-the-Ball   143
   Take Good Shots   146
   Protect the Ball   147
   Create Outnumbering Situations   148
   Maintain Proper Floor Balance   148
   Key Offensive Statistics   149
   Coach's Game Plan   150

11 Defensive Keys for Team Success   151
     ATTACK   153
     Essentials of Defense   153
     Sprint Back on Defense   154
     Talk on Defense   156
     Pressure the Ball   156
     Create Deflections   157
     Stop Dribble Penetration   159
     Keep the Ball Out of the Post Area   160
     Defend the Pick-and-Roll   160
     Contest All Shots   162
     Block Out   163
     Do Not Commit Unnecessary Fouls   164
     Key Defensive Statistics   165
     Coach's Game Plan   166

12 Winning Plays   167
     Baseline Out-of-Bounds Plays   168
     Sideline Out-of-Bounds Plays   175
     Half-Court Offense   179

Afterword   187

Glossary   190

References   194

Index   197

Foreword

From my first meeting with Coach Crean I realized Marquette was the right place for me. As I spent more time with him during the recruiting process I realized we shared a common vision on life. Admiration and appreciation are earned, and anything can be accomplished if you remain honest, modest, and humble.

The basketball program at Marquette is built on character, toughness, and unselfishness, a philosophy that everyone embodies from office workers to coaches. Each member of the team must put others before himself in order for the group to be successful. I learned this early on.

During my first year at Marquette I wasn't able to play in games because of my grades, but Coach Crean convinced me that I'd become a much better player through a year of practice. It was hard

Dwyane Wade visits with the media after Marquette's 83–69 victory over the number one ranked Kentucky Wildcats in the 2003 NCAA Regional Finals.

not being able to suit up on game day with my teammates, but it was the best thing that happened to me. I grew as a person and as a teammate. The conference championships and Final Four were great, and that first season was most memorable for me. It confirmed for me how special the program was.

Fifty years from now Marquette will still be my team. I'm proud to hear the words "Dwyane Wade from Marquette University" each time I'm introduced in NBA arenas. It reminds me of who I am and what I learned, but most importantly it reminds me of the people who shared the experience with me. With the support and guidance of Coach Crean and my teammates, I went from partial qualifier to 3.0 student, and from practice player to NBA All-Star.

Coaching Team Basketball is the perfect book for coaches and players to learn how to build cohesive teams where players place team goals first. There is nothing greater than being on a team where players truly care about each other. Unfortunately, these teams are rare because society places so much emphasis on individual play. Coach Crean and Coach Pim provide an easy-to-follow blueprint for team success. They have developed a system built on respect, responsibility, and teamwork. They select hard-working players who are committed to team play. They hold all team members accountable to the highest standard. Using their suggestions, your players can become a team of significance and enjoy the beauty of teamwork. Enjoy the journey and good luck!

—Dwyane Wade

Acknowledgments

Coaching Team Basketball would not have been possible without the contributions and support of many individuals. From start to finish, this book has been a team effort. Our deepest thanks go to:

Mark Weinstein, senior editor at McGraw-Hill, who believed in this project from the beginning and helped make it a reality.

Jenn Tust, senior project editor at McGraw-Hill, for her fine job managing the editorial processes that created the book you are holding.

Sharon Honaker for her excellent copyediting skills.

Jason Rabedeaux, Dan Panaggio, Jean Prioleau, Todd Townsend, and Derek Deprey, assistant basketball coaches, for their loyalty, great work ethic, sacrifice, and commitment to Marquette Basketball.

Barb Kellaher, special assistant to the head coach, for her attention to detail and supreme dedication.

Mike Broeker, associate athletic director, for providing the introduction and the great photography that appears in the book.

Scott Holsopple, head strength and conditioning coach, for his comprehensive strength, conditioning, and agility programs.

Hank Raymonds and Jack Harbaugh for sharing their timeless coaching wisdom.

Trey Schwab, outreach coordinator for organ procurement at the University of Wisconsin Hospital and Clinics, for demonstrating exceptional courage and commitment during his five years at Marquette.

Maj. Artie Coughlin, Dr. Lynn Fielitz, and Ed Fry for their outstanding help in compiling and analyzing the data to determine statistical variables that lead to winning or losing games in Division I basketball.

Maj. Derrick Stanton for producing the diagrams in this book and for his passion about the game of basketball.

Dean Lockwood, assistant basketball coach at the University of Tennessee, for his enthusiasm regarding the importance of this book and his insight on the extraordinary success of the Lady Vols.

Brig. Gen. (R) Maureen LeBoeuf for providing the opportunity to work at the nation's premier leadership institution.

Col. Gregory Daniels and Lt. Col. Jesse Germain, United States Military Academy, for their support and encouragement of this project.

Dr. Angela Lumpkin, professor of health, sport, and exercise science at the University of Kansas, and Lt. Col. Joe Doty at the United States Military Academy for reviewing *Coaching Team Basketball* and making invaluable suggestions that helped shape this book.

Maj. Ken Wanless and Maj. Joe Gelineau for their friendship and willingness to spend hours discussing the Army's approach to developing leaders of character.

Alma College: Where It All Began

It seems very fitting that Tom Crean and Ralph Pim should join forces again in the writing of *Coaching Team Basketball*. Their first joint effort was at Alma College in 1986 when Pim hired Crean as one of his assistants shortly after taking the head coaching position. Crean was a student at Central Michigan University at the time but that didn't deter Pim. "I hired Tom because of his passion for the game and his energy," said Pim. "He was the perfect addition to my staff because of his commitment and loyalty."

Crean will always remember the day that Pim gave him the opportunity to join Alma's staff. "I was only 20 years old at the time, and I couldn't believe that he was asking me to coach on the collegiate level," said Crean. "I first met Coach Pim when I was a teenager growing up in Mount Pleasant, Michigan, and he was coaching at Central Michigan University. He treated me with the same respect that he showed adults and spent hours answering my questions about coaching strategy, motivating athletes, and recruiting."

Along with Alma assistant coaches Rob Boden and Luke Stefanovsky, Crean and Pim inherited a losing program that needed a major overhaul. "Times were tough when Coach Pim and Coach Crean came into our program," said senior co-captain Scott Lewis. "It would have been easy for them to be influenced by what other people said about the returning players and not given us a chance. Instead, they said that everyone started with a clean slate, and those that worked and believed in the system would be rewarded."

"From the day we met Coach Pim in 1986, we bought into his vision and his goals for our program," said Pat Hengesbach, a three-year letter winner. By respecting the leader, everyone sacrificed for the good of the team and felt the role they played was important."

Crean and Pim built Alma's basketball program on desire, dedication, and discipline. Players were introduced to a system that pushed them beyond their preconceived limits. Scrimmages were not played with the normal basketball rules. There were no out-of-bounds lines and very few fouls called. One sportswriter described the scene as "players sliding across the gym floor and bouncing off the bleachers."

Dale Vos, current head coach at St. Clair County Community College and former Alma standout, remembers the intensity of the practices. "The number one thing I learned from Alma basketball was how to compete every day, every possession. The message from the coaches was very clear. When we stepped on the court, whether it was a practice, an open gym, or a game, it was time to compete. Nothing less than a player's best effort was accepted. I am still passionate about this today, and my staff and I are trying hard to pass this lesson on to the next generation of players."

All-Conference player Mark Bussell said, "Coach Pim and Coach Crean taught me the importance of striving for excellence with passion, purpose, and an unwavering commitment. I learned that excellence and success are anchored by strong character, integrity, attitude, and hard work. I also learned that adversity is a part of life and how you react to difficult times ultimately determines your success or failure."

Their initial campaign produced Alma's first winning season in seven years and a banner recruiting class. Crean quickly distinguished himself as an outstanding recruiter. Four members of the incoming recruiting class participated in the Michigan High School All-Star Game. "Tom was great at identifying hard-nosed players that fit into our system," said Pim. "He was a relentless recruiter and was responsible for signing 12 All-State players during our three years."

Players were taught the importance of team togetherness both on and off the court. "I fondly think of my teammates and coaches as if we are all brothers," said Bussell. "Through the wins and losses, we grew together as a family. In fact, the unbelievable bond among team members is still strong today."

Alma's basketball program reached even greater success during the next two years and earned the respect of basketball fans throughout Michigan. Crean and Pim led Alma to national rankings in three-point field goals and points scored, and the 1989 squad recorded the school's best overall record in 47 years.

After the 1989 season, Pim and Crean left Alma. Pim accepted new challenges at the College of William and Mary while Crean joined

Jud Heathcote's staff at Michigan State University. Even though their years together at Alma were short, the impact they made on their players and on each other was significant.

"I walked into the gym in 1987 as an 18-year-old kid, and, by the time Ralph Pim and Tom Crean left after my sophomore year, I had made great strides toward becoming a responsible adult," said Jerry Czarnecki. "Much of my success since college has been the direct result of the seeds planted during those two years."

"Whether it is life, business, or family, I owe much of my success to my Alma College teammates and coaches," said Bussell. "As a father, my greatest wish is for my children to have an opportunity for a similar experience with coaches like the ones I played for at Alma—individuals like Coach Pim and Coach Crean, who truly care about the development of young people."

"As I look back, it was a pivotal time in my life," said Lewis. "I was coming off the death of my mother, a lady who because of her self-less service still drives me as a person today. The coaches at Alma helped instill the courage it takes to be a leader. I can recall the very play, game, and loss that it occurred in. We were behind by one point with five seconds remaining. Coach Pim set up a play for me to take the game-winning shot. I quickly dribbled across the midcourt line, but instead of shooting, I passed to a wide-open teammate in the corner and the ball went through his hands and out of bounds as time expired.

"As we jogged off the court, Coach Pim approached me with a very passionate, but classy lesson. He said, 'Lewie, I don't care if it is a 40-footer, you take that shot.' From that day on, I understood what Coach was telling me. I earned the right for that shot and should have taken it. That's what a leader does. Sometimes you need to lose by one point to learn a lesson that changes your life."

Crean often thinks back to his years at Alma College. "It was a great experience for me, and I will never forget the coaches and players," he said. "I learned from Coach Pim that the greatest thing a coach can do is to prepare his or her players for life after their playing days are over. He wanted players to learn more from the game than just skills. I treasure the memories of our three years together, and I can never repay him for the opportunities he provided. Coach Pim has always been an important mentor to me."

Pim loves watching the success of his former assistant. "Tom has risen to the top of the coaching profession because he never stops learning," said Pim. "He seeks out the best and is always looking for ways to improve. Tom's enthusiasm and determination are unmatched. He is a master at getting the most from his players. I am very, very proud of him."

—Michael Broeker, athletic director,
Marquette University

Key to Diagrams

Offensive player	1, 2, 3, 4, 5
Offensive player with the ball	(1)
Defensive player	X
Pass (and direction)	----------▶
Dribble	〜〜〜〜▶
Screen or pick	———┤
Player movement	——————▶
"V" cut	╲╱▶

Symbols are used to make the diagrams easy to read. The three-point line shown in the diagrams is the college distance used during the 2006 season.

1

Teamwork

Teamwork is really a form of trust. It's what happens when you surrender the mistaken idea that you can go it alone and realize that you won't achieve your individual goals without the support of your colleagues.

—Pat Summitt, Naismith Basketball Hall of Fame Coach

For a team to succeed, there must be trust and respect between all team members.

1

Where Has the Team Play Gone?

On most every campus, there are players thinking about making it to the NBA, rather than making their teams and teammates better.

—Jay Bilas, ESPN College Basketball Analyst

Dr. James Naismith invented basketball in 1891 at Springfield College as a way of providing exercise and enjoyment for students during the long New England winters. The game was an instant success because it was fun and competitive, and it required teamwork. Not long after his invention Naismith proclaimed, "In basketball there is no place for the egotist." Naismith might be disappointed if he watched the lack of team play that characterizes many games today.

Today, many basketball experts are asking, "Where has the team play gone?" The game is more popular today than ever before, but the spotlight has shifted from team play and selflessness to individual play and personal acclaim. It has been a long time since young players modeled themselves after superstars, such as Bill Russell, who placed their teams above individual glory and statistics. Russell led the Boston Celtics to 11 NBA championships in 13 years.

Championships are not won unless a team has forged in a high degree of unity, attainable only through the selflessness of each of its players.

—Bill Bradley, Naismith Basketball Hall of Fame Player

Russell was a guest at Marquette's Midnight Madness in 2003 and spoke to the players about the importance of teamwork. He explained that playing for the team was a way of life for the Boston Celtics. Each Celtic player learned that in order to earn a spot, he had to be willing to "give himself up" for the good of the team.

Russell described himself as one of the most egotistical players that anyone would ever meet, but he differentiated his ego from the egos of many of today's players. "My ego is not a personal ego," stated Russell, "it's a team ego. My ego demands for myself, the success of my team. My personal achievement became my team achievement."

The New Generation

Many players in the millennial generation do not believe in Russell's "team ego" theory, and basketball is becoming an expression of self rather than team. Today's players are growing up in a culture that promotes individual stars. They watch their sport heroes living a celebrity's lifestyle where self-centeredness is the norm and instant gratification is a top priority.

Players and fans celebrate spectacular individual performances and often miss the beauty of five players working together. In the aftermath of Los Angeles Laker Kobe Bryant's amazing 81-point scoring night against the Toronto Raptors in 2006, NBA all-star Vince Carter warned young players not to be overly influenced by Bryant's scoring exploits. He encouraged them to honor the team concept first. "That is what is missing in the game, guys understanding how to play as a team," said Carter.

Legendary Hall of Fame player Oscar Robertson believes all the attention given to Bryant's scoring spree exemplifies the focus of the NBA today on individual statistics instead of team success. "As far as I'm concerned," Robertson said, "the only stat that counts is the win column. To be on top in that category, you have to play team basketball. You can't have just one or two players taking all the shots."

Today, the signature move in basketball is the slam dunk, which fans relate to as a declaration of power and dominance. This throw-it-down, in-your-face move is symbolic of the direction that basketball is heading. Many players are choosing style over substance, and the beauty of teamwork is slowly vanishing from the playgrounds and gymnasiums across our nation.

The Decline of U.S. Men's Basketball

U.S. basketball once stood at the pinnacle of the basketball world. From basketball's inclusion in the Olympic Games in 1936 to 2000, the United States compiled a spectacular 109-2 record. The losses came in 1972, during a controversial loss to the Soviet Union, and in 1988, when Hall of Fame coach John Thompson took the last group of exclusively college players to the Olympics and were beaten by an older and more experienced team from the Soviet Union.

The results from the 2004 Olympic Games verified that the USA Men's Basketball Team was no longer the giant of the basketball world. The Americans were outplayed and beaten by nations that showcased fundamental basketball and team play. The USA team lost three times in 13 days and went home with a third-place finish and the bronze medal. The fear factor of playing the United States in any international basketball competition no longer exists.

The upsetting point about the U.S. Olympic decline is that it is not a question of raw talent. Fran Fraschilla, ESPN analyst and international basketball expert, believes the underlying issue is the evolution over the past couple of decades to a "me-first, highlights-driven style of play" in the United States. "It has compromised our ability to play team basketball," said Fraschilla, "which is really impacting the quality of the game in the U.S."

Fraschilla is not alone in his views. Many basketball experts believe that team play has become an endangered species in men's basketball. One of these is legendary coach John Wooden. His UCLA teams reached unprecedented heights that will be difficult for any team to match. The Bruins set all-time records with four perfect 30-0 seasons, 88 consecutive victories, 38 straight NCAA tournament victories, 20 conference championships, and 10 NCAA national championships, including 7 in a row.

After the 2004 Olympics, Wooden said he thought the United States would win because of the athletic abilities of its players and the expertise of U.S. Olympic coach Larry Brown. But as Wooden watched the games, he thought the players demonstrated too much "me" and not enough "we." "That's the way they (NBA players) have learned to play," Wooden said. "The NBA loves showmanship. That's what their fans want. But in the Olympics it's about the team, not the individual."

Coach Brown acknowledged the decline of the American game and pointed out some deficiencies in today's players. "When I was growing up," said Brown, "the first thing players used to do was throw the ball inside, trying to draw fouls or make easy baskets. Great players like Michael Jordan, Larry Bird, and Magic Johnson understood this from the beginning of their careers, but it's going to take some time for the current generation of players to understand this concept."

Differences Between U.S. and Foreign Players

There are distinct differences between the styles of play between U.S. and foreign players. American players often try to make spectacular plays while foreign players prefer to penetrate and pass to open teammates. As a result, foreign players demonstrate more of a team game with five players working together to create the best shot. This is very different from the American style that highlights two-man plays and often results in three players standing on the perimeter watching the action.

Kelvin Sampson, Indiana's highly successful coach and veteran of international competition, thinks that foreign players rely more on team basketball. "American players play in a crowd and shoot shots with a higher degree of difficulty," said Sampson. "They get by their defender, drive to the basket, and then try to jump over their opponent. They want to make the great play. On the other hand, foreign players maintain excellent spacing and avoid playing in a crowd. They draw the defense and then pass to an open teammate."

Dan Panaggio, assistant coach at Marquette, spent four years as an assistant coach with the Portland Trail Blazers and recognized a difference in the mind-set of foreign players regarding teamwork. "I tend to agree with many people in the NBA who believe that it is easier to build team chemistry using foreign players who have not been pampered in the AAU system or spoiled by the limelight of Division I basketball," stated Panaggio.

Another difference between American and foreign players is the respect shown to coaches. Too often we see American players arguing with coaches or publicly demonstrating disgust with a coach's decision. Donnie Nelson, president of operations for the Dallas Mavericks, helped build basketball in the country of Lithuania and witnessed a higher level of reverence for coaches abroad. "In most other countries, coaching is revered and respected," stated Nelson. "In our country now, it's tolerated. I don't know all the reasons for that, but when people fill a young player's head with garbage and tell him he's the next Michael Jordan when he's not, and that player listens to what the media says about them, they stop working on their games. We have to recapture the way we teach players."

The Influence of the NBA

No longer is it the norm for talented players to play four years of college basketball. Most superstars leave their college campuses for the NBA after one or two years. In the 2004 NBA draft, 25 of the first 29 picks were not college seniors. ESPN college basketball analyst Jay Bilas believes this has created a major problem because players are spending more time thinking about the next step into the NBA and less time concentrating on becoming a better team player.

"Coaching is tougher than it has ever been," said Bilas. "The NBA has distorted everything in college and high school basketball, and it has been a nightmare for college coaches. On most every campus, there are players thinking about making it to the NBA, rather than making their teams and teammates better. When a coach tries to teach or gives an assignment, the player is often more concerned about how it will affect his development and his timetable for making it to the league (NBA)."

The NBA's marketing of individual stars rather than teams has also had an impact on today's players. Veteran coach George Karl said, "It was never the Seattle Supersonics playing the Los Angeles Lakers. It was always (Gary) Payton vs. (Shaquille) O'Neal. Very seldom do you hear people talk about team assists and fundamentals."

Where Does Basketball Go from Here?

Men's basketball in the United States is at a crossroads. The gauntlet has officially been dropped. The United States finished sixth in the 2002 World Championships, and they were embarrassed on the Olympic stage in 2004. It is time to examine our basketball's system and make the necessary changes if we want to establish a new level of excellence as it relates to the rest of the world.

Duke head coach Mike Krzyzewski has been selected head coach of the USA Men's Basketball Team for the 2008 Olympics. He has emphatically stated that he will select talented, committed team players who want to represent their country. "When you look up at the scoreboard, it will say the United States," Krzyzewski said. "It will never say an individual name. I can promise you, we will put together a team that will serve as an example to the rest of the world of the way the game should be played and the way you should conduct yourself."

The focal point must be a return to team basketball. Every coach on every level can make a difference by helping players understand the importance of team play and holding players accountable to the tenets of teamwork. Five players working together as a single unit should be the standard. A team can ascend to amazing heights when each player regards the name on the front of his or her jersey as more important than the name on the back.

In order to have a winner, the team must have a feeling of unity; every player must put the team first—ahead of personal glory.

—Paul "Bear" Bryant, Legendary Alabama Football Coach

An Application Model for Team Play

Basketball is the greatest team game in the world, but the concept of being part of a team eludes many of today's players in the United States. *Coaching Team Basketball* presents a model that can be used by basketball coaches to build strong teams. It describes a system that facilitates empowerment, accountability, and teamwork. It includes tips from some of the game's greatest coaches, lessons from basketball-power Marquette University, and stories about Dwyane Wade's magnificent rise to NBA stardom.

The book provides activities to assist coaches in building value-based programs. There are lessons from the U.S. Army and the United States Military Academy to help develop leaders of character, dozens of important teaching points and game-winning plays, and self-assessments. The offensive and defensive keys to success are discussed plus statistical evidence is provided that highlights the most important factors in creating a winning team in basketball. Each chapter includes powerful quotes and concludes with an Instant Replay or summary of key points.

Coaching Team Basketball has been written for younger coaches who aspire to be great team builders; experienced head coaches who mentor assistant coaches; and players so they can experience the miracles that occur when a group of individuals combine their strengths to achieve feats of lasting significance.

It's time to put your game face on and begin the journey!

Instant Replay

1. An appreciation for the beauty of teamwork is slowly vanishing from the playgrounds and gymnasiums.
2. Young players are growing up in a culture that promotes individual stars rather than teams.
3. The spotlight has shifted from team play to showmanship.
4. The United States no longer reigns supreme in the world of basketball.
5. The purpose of *Coaching Team Basketball* is to provide an application model that promotes teamwork and helps individuals excel in the team environment.

2
Teamwork Trumps Individual Talent

Teams that play together beat those with superior players who play more as individuals.

—Jack Ramsay, Naismith Basketball Hall of Fame Coach

Teamwork separates winners and losers. No collection of players, no matter how talented, can win unless they form a team. The word *team* is an acronym for a dominant truth: Together Everyone Achieves More. We suggest changing the last word from *more* to *miracles* because exceptional team play can result in extraordinary feats. No dream is out of reach for a smooth-functioning team.

Miracle on Ice

A perfect case in point is the gold medal U.S. Hockey Team in the 1980 Winter Games. This team of amateur and collegiate players defeated the Soviet Union against near-impossible odds.

The United States entered the Olympics seeded seventh in the final round of 12 teams and had been crushed by the Soviet Union in an exhibition match at Madison Square Garden only weeks earlier. The day before the match, columnist Dave Anderson wrote in the *New York Times*, "Unless the ice melts, or unless the United States Team or another team performs a miracle . . . the Russians are expected to win the Olympic gold medal for the sixth time in the last seven tournaments."

Herb Brooks, coach of the U.S. team, was hockey's version of George Patton or Norman Schwarzkopf. He was a combination dictator-philosopher who forced his players to think and act like a team. Brooks convinced his players that together they could overcome all obstacles. Brooks selected team members who possessed qualities that he admired most. "The players had big egos," said Brooks, "but they didn't have ego problems. That's why all-star teams traditionally seem to self-destruct. We didn't."

Players kept a notebook of what they called "Brooksisms." One of them was: "This team isn't talented enough to win on talent alone."

Before the game against the Soviet Union, Brooks pulled out a note card and read, "You were born to be a player. You were meant to be here." His players believed him and went on to upset the Russians 4–3.

As the game ended, ABC broadcaster Al Michaels gave his exuberant, impromptu call: "Five seconds left in the game. Four left in the game. Do you believe in miracles? YES!! Unbelievable!"

In order for the power of teamwork to take place, as it did in the 1980 Winter Games, two elements are necessary. First, individual team members must share a common objective, one that is important enough to them that they are willing to make sacrifices in order to achieve it. Second, team members must care for each other in a way that eventually leads to selflessness.

Dynasty of the 1990s

In leading the Chicago Bulls to six NBA championships in eight years, Coach Phil Jackson built a dynasty on the core values of self-lessness and compassion. He believed that our society has placed such a high premium on individual achievement that it is easy for NBA players to get blinded by their own self-importance. They lose a sense of interconnectedness with their teammates because their primary focus is on individual glory. These athletes fail to grasp the concept that team play does not overshadow individual strengths; it enhances them and greatly improves a team's chance for success. Using a passage from Rudyard Kipling's *Second Jungle Book* as his model, Jackson said, "The strength of the team is each individual member; the strength of each member is the team."

The challenge that coaches on all levels face is how to get team members to give themselves wholeheartedly to the group effort and put the team first. Highly successful coaches teach their players the power of selflessness because they believe in the adage "the surest way to happiness is to lose yourself in a cause greater than you."

Jackson believed the best way to teach selflessness was to create a team on which every player had a vital role. His vision was to use 10 players regularly and give the remaining players enough playing time so they could fit in with the others. A key component of his system was the triangle offense designed by Assistant Coach Tex Winter.

Jackson knew this particular offense would work only if star player Michael Jordan gave up the ball more, took fewer shots, and scored fewer points. Jackson told Jordan that he probably would not win his fourth straight scoring title but that the team would be much better. Jordan initially had doubts, but he devoted himself to learning the system. In a short period of time, Jordan realized that the triangle offense allowed him to fit into the flow of the offense and to accentuate the talents of his teammates. As a result, selflessness and teamwork transformed the Bulls from contenders to world champions.

"There are plenty of teams in every sport that have great players and never win titles," said Jordan. "Most of the time, those players aren't willing to sacrifice for the greater good of the team. The funny thing is, in the end, their unwillingness to sacrifice only makes individual goals more difficult to achieve. One thing I believe to the fullest is that if you think and achieve as a team, the individual accolades will take care of themselves. Talent wins games, but teamwork and intelligence win championships."

Selflessness was the key factor in Chicago's last possession of the 1993 NBA Finals. Trailing the Phoenix Suns by two points with 14 seconds remaining, the Bulls had possession of the ball. Chicago's strategy was to get the ball to Jordan in the open court and have him penetrate to the basket. Phoenix countered by double-teaming Michael as soon as he received the ball. Instead of forcing the action, Jordan passed to Scottie Pippen. As Pippen drove to the basket, he saw that Horace Grant was open on the left side and delivered an accurate pass. Grant looked over his right shoulder and found sharpshooter Jim Paxson open on the perimeter. Paxson caught the ball and quickly swished one of his patented three-point shots for the victory. Five Chicago players touched the ball during the last 14 seconds, and each one read the defense, found an open teammate, and unselfishly gave up the ball so the team would be successful.

The Model Franchise in the NFL

The New England Patriots, under Coach Bill Belichick, won the Super Bowl in 2002, 2004, and 2005. They became the model franchise in the NFL not because they had the best players, but because of their team-first attitude. Week after week, the Patriots defeated opponents because the 11 players on the field worked as one powerful unit. They played at a high level of intensity, did what they were supposed to do, and did not make many mental mistakes.

Coaches in all sports can learn valuable lessons from the New England Patriots on how to build teams that maximize the strengths of all their players. A key component of Belichick's philosophy is collective responsibility. He believes a player's primary focus must be on doing what he can to help the team win. Quarterback Tom Brady said, "In football, you're entirely dependent upon the guys you're with. Ultimately, the pride and the enjoyment come from succeeding as a group. It's about how you can try to get everyone else doing the right thing so they can rise to that level, too."

The mind-set of the New England Patriots is not the norm in today's professional sports world. Many teams are driven by the egos of a few star players. The team prospers when their star players are happy, but the team quickly crumbles when the superstars become dissatisfied. During the course of any season, it is common to read newspaper accounts of how star players are disenchanted and feel their talents could be better used on another team.

"As I surveyed the dysfunctional landscape of sports in recent days, with its flying fists, stun guns, dropping towels, and BCS equations," said Richard Oliver of the *San Antonio Express-News*, "I found myself seeking out the kind of old-school, rock-solid franchise that recalled life before Terrell Owens. I appreciated, once again, the New England Patriots. A team that always seems to avoid notice, but commands admiration. A team not defined by any one individual, but by a collection of individuals with singular purpose."

The main ingredient of stardom is the rest of the team.

—John Wooden, Naismith Basketball Hall of Fame Player and Coach

Princeton: "The Little Engine That Could"

Coach Pete Carril took a chapter from the classic book *The Little Engine That Could* and taught his Princeton players the power of teamwork and perseverance. Carril's players beat teams composed of superior athletes by playing together and adhering to an offensive system featuring exceptional passing, shooting, and backdoor cuts. The key component in Carril's successful scheme was unselfish players. "I look for players who realize the world doesn't revolve around them," said Carril.

Few coaches have ever achieved more with less than Carril. He was the first Division I coach to win more than five hundred games with no athletic scholarships. In Carril's last season at Princeton, the Tigers were matched against defending national champions UCLA in the first round of the NCAA tournament. UCLA looked like they were in control with a seven-point lead with six minutes to play, but Princeton came charging back with a three-point basket and two layups. With the score tied and only 3.8 seconds remaining, Princeton executed their patented backdoor layup for a stunning 43–41 victory.

When a team outgrows individual performance and learns team confidence, excellence becomes a reality.

—Joe Paterno, Legendary Penn State Football Coach

There Is No "I" in Team

The power of teamwork took Marquette University to the NCAA Final Four in 2003. A national sportswriter asked Bill Cords, athletic director at Marquette, whether Marquette's appearance was an aberration or an anomaly. Cords quickly said, "It's neither one. It is a great example of what people can do if they are all on the same page, have the same expectations, and are all committed to success."

The road to the Final Four in New Orleans was not a smooth one for the Marquette Golden Eagles. There were potholes, precarious bends, and detours along the way. Each member of the team had to demonstrate a willingness to sacrifice personal goals so team goals could be reached. In other words, players had to learn there is no "I" in team.

"We didn't have the most talented players at Marquette," said Travis Diener, second-round pick of the Orlando Magic in the 2005 NBA draft. "But we did have players that truly cared about each other. We did everything within our power never to let a fellow teammate down. The closeness of the team both on and off the court allowed us to overcome any challenge that was placed in our path."

One of those critical challenges occurred on January 7, 2003. Marquette had lost back-to-back road games and was facing Saint Louis in a pivotal game on the latter's home court. Marquette superstar Dwyane Wade was knocked to the floor as he drove to the basket and

"Going to the Final Four in 2003 is a great example of what a team can do when every team member is committed to success."

—Bill Cords, Athletic Director, Marquette University

had to leave the game. He was taken to the locker room, iced, and examined by doctors. In the meantime, Marquette's players rallied together and refused to allow Wade's absence to affect the outcome of the game. Travis Diener stepped up and emerged as a leader. Scott Merritt had a team-high 14 points, and Steve Novak scored 10 big points in the second half to help lead the Golden Eagles to a six-point victory.

Wade returned late in the game, despite his badly bruised ribs, and totally immersed himself into doing whatever it took for his team to win. Wade scored only six points, but he wasn't concerned about his personal statistics. The only thing that mattered was that Marquette won. He put the team ahead of any personal glory and looked for ways to make his teammates better.

"Making my teammates better doesn't necessarily have anything to do with me being in the game," said Wade. "It can come in a lot of different areas. It could be attending study hall if someone needs a study partner, spending time with a teammate. It's doing a lot of things. On the court I think I do a pretty good job of making my teammates better by passing the ball and giving them confidence to shoot."

"Great things happen if you always play hard, stay focused on your goals, and do everything within your power to help your teammates be successful."

—Travis Diener,
Three-Time All-Conference USA selection

The media and fans often give their attention to the leading scorer, but, in reality, the game's outcome is determined by team play. "I don't judge myself by how many points I score," said Diener. "I judge my success on whether I controlled the tempo of the game and got the ball to the right people at the right times, and our team won."

In the reception area of the Marquette basketball office, a prominent sign reads: On a Team, Everyone Makes a Difference. These seven words are the backbone for team togetherness. Bonds have to form among all members of the team—head coach to player, player to player, player to manager, head coach to assistant coach, assistant coach to assistant coach, administrative assistant to head coach, strength coach to players, and so on. To succeed, every individual must have a trusting relationship with every other member of the team.

One Team, One Fight

Successful basketball coaches adhere to the "one team, one fight" model. This concept originates from one of the most important traditions in the Army. It is the belief that success comes from an integrated approach. All units and divisions are part of a joint team. Everyone must do his or her job, no matter how big or small, in order for the team to be successful.

This point was emphasized in a speech delivered by Colin Powell to his staff soon after he became secretary of state. "There is no job in the State Department that is unimportant," declared Powell. "I believe that everybody has a vital role to play, and it is my job to communicate and convey down through every layer to the last person in the organization, the valuable role that they are performing and how . . . they contribute to the mission. We have to be linked."

Coach Dean Smith's basketball program at North Carolina is an example of the "one team, one fight" model. It was built on the tenets of integrity, honor, respect, and loyalty, and it fostered team togetherness and camaraderie. Smith did not differentiate between the lesser-skilled and higher-skilled athletes. "Whether you were a starter or a 12th man, he made us all feel like we were the most important player who ever played for him," remembered Larry Brown, former player and Hall of Fame coach.

Pat Riley created the motto "15 Strong" during Miami's 2006 NBA championship season. It emphasized the importance of every player in the overall success of the team. Riley reinforced this by producing business cards with "15 Strong" on one side and an image of the NBA championship trophy on the other.

Teamwork Must Be Taught

Teaching teamwork is one of today's greatest challenges in coaching because players have grown up in a society that does not emphasize sharing. Often, players have their own agenda because their focus is centered on what's in it for them. They want to know what they are going to get from the team, rather than asking what they can do to make the team better.

"Team togetherness, both on the court and off the court, is stressed the moment you arrive on campus."

—Steve Novak, 2006 First Team
All-Big East Conference selection

Teamwork must be the central focus every day of the year in everything that is done. No team will succeed without teamwork, no matter how many All-Americans it has. "You constantly have to teach team basketball," Dan Panaggio said. "You have to insist that players work together, and you cannot accept poor results."

The number one killer of team play is dissension from within. Many coaches focus too much attention on evaluating their opponents rather than making sure their own team is harmonious. The bottom line is that a team must learn how to function effectively and efficiently so that, individually and collectively, the members of the team can attain their goals.

Selfless Service

The essence of teamwork is selfless service. At the United States Military Academy, team building begins on a cadet's arrival, called Reception Day. In June of every year, more than 1,100 individuals

"To be successful in our program, a player must learn how to be unselfish and play the role that is needed."

—Marcus Jackson,
Marquette University letter winner 2004–05

begin a 47-month journey with the goal of being a "commissioned leader of character committed to the values of Duty, Honor, and Country."

New cadets quickly learn that survival in basic training is based on team incentives. Team members must work together and maximize their strengths. Cadets begin to understand that being part of a group makes each individual more powerful and at the same time, elevates the team to the point where the whole is greater than the sum of its parts.

This phenomenon is often referred to as synergy. Synergy is the power of teamwork that combines individual strengths to compensate for individual shortcomings so that more and greater feats can be accomplished. Author Stephen Covey described synergy in mathematical terms as $1 + 1 = 3$ or more.

Marquette's point guard Dominic James spoke about the importance of teamwork early in his college career. After dishing out eight assists in the semifinals of the Great Alaska Shootout, James said,

"We've just got to keep playing together and emphasizing that if we do that, we can get to the places we need to be." Marquette beat South Carolina in overtime to win the tournament title for the second time in the last four years. Steve Novak was selected the Most Outstanding Player of the tournament while James and fellow freshman guard Jerel McNeal were voted on the All-Tournament Team.

The Detroit Pistons reigned as the 2004 NBA Champions because their sum was far stronger than their individual parts. The Pistons soundly defeated the Los Angeles Lakers, one of the most glamorous collections of superstars ever, because Coach Larry Brown got his players to play the game "his way." Brown believed all successful teams have three characteristics: "they play unselfish, they play together, and they play hard."

Joe Dumars, Detroit's president of basketball operations, agreed that team play was the deciding factor in the championship series. "I knew that they (Los Angeles) had the two best players in the world (Shaquille O'Neal and Kobe Bryant), but this is not a tennis match, it is basketball," stated Dumars.

> *Winning teams at the NBA level, the college level, and the high school level all play team basketball. Championship teams have five players on the same page at all times.*
>
> —Hubie Brown, Naismith Basketball Hall of Fame Coach

Synergy is always a fragile balance between the team member and the team. Even the slightest action can upset the chemistry of a team. It can be something as simple as a quote in a newspaper article or a meaningless prank played on a teammate. Coaches must always be on the lookout for threats to their team's togetherness.

A Team Wins and Loses Together

John Wooden was a "philosopher-coach" whose teachings went far beyond the dimensions of a basketball court. One of his greatest insights was that a team must not only win as a team but also lose as a team. Wooden understood that after a loss it would be easy for those players that did not play to feel they were not responsible for the outcome. He made sure that all team members felt a part of everything that happened to the team whether it was good or bad. The powerful bonds among players held Wooden's teams together. He constantly focused on the group and made sure that all his players knew that there could be no success unless everybody put the welfare of the team ahead of personal glory.

An example of a team that demonstrated collective responsibility after a loss occurred on February 26, 1989, when Arizona defeated Duke 77–75. With one second remaining and Arizona ahead by two points, Duke's freshman Christian Laettner was fouled and went to the free throw line to shoot a one-and-one. His first shot hit the back of the rim and bounced into the hands of an Arizona player. As the buzzer sounded, Duke's senior captains Danny Ferry and Quin Snyder and the rest of the Duke team raced over to a dejected Laettner and put their arms around him. Every player felt Laettner's pain. There were no excuses, finger pointing, or team members laying on the floor in disappointment. The entire team held themselves accountable for the outcome of the game rather than blaming the player that missed the last shot.

Instant Replay

1. No organization will succeed without teamwork.
2. Team play does not overshadow individual strengths, it enhances them.
3. Players must learn there is no "I" in team.
4. Every member of an organization is an important cog in the program.
5. Division from within destroys a team's success more than any opponent.
6. Teamwork must be taught and nurtured every day.

3

The Meaning of Team Play

Basketball is a beautiful game when the five players on the court play with one heartbeat.

—Dean Smith, Naismith Basketball Hall of Fame Coach

Today, many players do not have a clear picture of what team basketball looks like on the court or what their role should be in making it happen. One reason is because they have grown up watching ESPN highlights that showcase dazzling individual play. Very seldom do the clips illustrate the teamwork that must take place to produce teams of excellence. As a result, many players correlate success with individual brilliance.

Ultimately, it is the responsibility of the head coach to demand that team basketball occurs. This is one of the most difficult tasks for a coach because a player's perception of teamwork may be a far cry from reality. Oscar Robertson thinks many moderately skilled players really believe they are stars and the team revolves around them. The best place to begin is to describe the qualities of a team player.

Qualities of a Team Player

A team player is a person that uses his or her ability to fit into a system that enables a group of players to accomplish more than any one individual could alone. Team players understand that teamwork is an essential ingredient in championship teams. They hold themselves responsible for being a good team player and are always looking for ways to improve. Team members should continually assess their actions. Located in the Coach's Game Plan at the end of this chapter, Activity 3.1 is a self-assessment designed to help players identify their strengths and weaknesses as a team player.

> *Teamwork is not a matter of persuading yourself and your colleagues to set aside personal ambitions for the greater good. It's a matter of recognizing that your personal ambitions and the ambitions of the team are one and the same.*
>
> —Pat Summitt, Naismith Basketball Hall of Fame Coach

Exemplary team players have four common qualities. First and foremost, they place the success of the team ahead of individual goals and personal glory. A great example of a player placing team success ahead of personal glory occurred during Marquette's 2005 season. Guard Travis Diener was fast approaching the school's all-time scoring record when he was sidelined by a season-ending injury. When asked about the scoring record, Diener responded, "The scoring record really didn't mean that much to me. George Thompson was a great player and did a lot of wonderful things, and he set the record

"I always want to be remembered as a winner and a player that never let his teammates down."

—Travis Diener, Second Round selection of the Orlando Magic in the 2005 NBA Draft

in three years. He deserves to be in that top spot. The personal goal that I wanted most would have been to be the player that participated in the most number of wins during his Marquette career."

Another example of a player that placed the team above personal glory occurred in December 2005 when Marquette freshman standout Wesley Matthews fractured his right foot and missed eight Big East Conference games. Matthews had been in the midst of his most productive stretch of the season, having scored a collegiate-high 21 points against Oakland and grabbing 13 rebounds against Lewis. Instead of feeling sorry for himself, Matthews turned his focus to the success of the team. "It's a team sport," said Matthews. "It's not about me. You've got to get past the self-pity and move on to helping the team win games. The season's not over, and it's not over for me."

Create unselfishness as the most important team attribute.

—Bill Russell, Naismith Basketball Hall of Fame Player

The second quality of exemplary team players is trust and respect, the core ingredients of teamwork. Duke coach Mike Krzyzewski said, "It is amazing what can be accomplished when all individuals involved trust one another. The best way to turn a crisis into a success is to have a group of people who trust one another."

Exemplary team players trust their teammates and have confidence in their playing abilities. This was the case in Game Six of the 1997 NBA Finals between the Chicago Bulls and the Utah Jazz. Bulls coach Phil Jackson drew up a play for Michael Jordan during the last time-out. But as the team broke the huddle, Jordan told teammate Steve Kerr to be ready to shoot an open jump shot. Jordan proved to be a prophet because Kerr's defender came over to help on Jordan. Jordan didn't hesitate to throw the ball to Kerr for the shot that clinched the title for the Bulls. Team players do not force shots. They trust their teammates and get the ball in the hands of open shooters.

In 2006, senior Joe Chapman played a key role in Marquette's upset over nationally ranked Georgetown when he hit a three-pointer from deep in the right corner with 2:31 remaining and the Golden Eagles down by one point. After the game, teammate Steve Novak said, "Joe Chapman has stepped up all year. There's no question that everyone on the team has faith in him. When he hit that shot with the score 49–48, it was a huge boost for us."

You develop a team to achieve what one person cannot accomplish alone. All of us alone are weaker, by far, than if all of us are together.

—Mike Krzyzewski, Naismith Basketball Hall of Fame Coach

"I want championships, not scoring titles or MVPs. . . . My job is to give my teammates confidence."

—Dwyane Wade, Miami Heat,
2006 NBA Champions

The third quality of exemplary team players is they make every team member a better performer. This is NBA superstar Dwyane Wade's most important quality as a basketball player. He thoroughly understands how to make the right pass at the right time in order to provide scoring opportunities for his teammates. He always plays with his head up. As simple as this may sound, it is very hard to do. Wade is constantly looking for an open teammate.

Taking care of teammates is the fourth quality of exemplary team players. They refuse to let a team member fail. When they sense a teammate is down, they help that person get back on his or her feet. A good example of this occurred after Game One of the NBA 2005 Eastern Conference Finals. Detroit had defeated Miami 90–81 and forced Wade into one of the poorer performances of his career. The next day Shaquille O'Neal and Alonzo Mourning came over to Wade's home. They wanted to check on their teammate and let him know that they cared.

This act of concern went a long way with Wade. "I think one of the biggest things that helped me was that Zo and Shaq came and picked me up," said Wade. "We went for a little ride and talked. We all have one goal in mind. We all want to win a championship. I listen to guys who have been doing it for years, and I just try to come out and make them proud. That's what this team is all about. Anytime someone is struggling, someone is down, there's always guys that will pick you up. That's why we have something special here with the Heat."

Wade responded in Game Two with 40 points, eight rebounds, six assists, and two blocks in Miami's 92–86 victory.

Vince Lombardi, legendary coach of the Green Bay Packers, said, "If you're going to play together as a team, you've got to care for one another. You've got to love each other. Each player has to be thinking about the next guy and saying to himself, 'If I don't block that man, my teammate's going to get his legs broken. I have to do my job well so that my teammates can do theirs.' The difference between mediocrity and greatness is the feeling these guys have for each other."

Teamwork is what the Green Bay Packers were all about. They didn't do it for individual glory. They did it because they loved one another.

—Vince Lombardi, NFL Championship Coach

Never letting a teammate down is something that is talked about almost every day at Marquette. Players are held accountable for making their teammates successful. "We quickly learn if one player isn't doing his job, then he is hurting the whole team," said Travis Diener. "In our program no one wants to bring the team down."

Role Models for Team Play

Effective coaches identify role models for their players to emulate. Two excellent examples are former NBA great Bill Russell and current superstar Wade.

Bill Russell

Bill Russell was selected the "Twentieth Century's Greatest Team Player" by *Sports Illustrated*, and Home Box Office recognized him as "The Greatest Winner of the Twentieth Century." Within a one-year time frame, Russell won an NCAA championship, an Olympic gold medal, and an NBA championship. His career was not about personal statistics, MVP awards, or endorsements. Russell never played for the fans or the limelight. He was focused on one thing—team championships.

At the University of San Francisco, Russell led the Dons to back-to-back NCAA national championships. "I realized at a young age that individual awards were mostly political," said Russell. "But with winning and losing there were no politics, only numbers. I decided that the only really important thing was to try and win every game. And to win regularly, I would have to subordinate my individual goals so my team would be able to win. As a result, I became the kind of leader who understood that doing the most for my team would best guarantee success."

Russell led the Boston Celtics to 11 NBA championships, including 8 consecutive titles from 1959 to 1966. The Celtic players from those championship teams helped design rings that symbolized their excellence. On those precious gems are two words—*teamwork* and *pride*.

"What I found with the Celtics was a set of other players who were brilliant and accomplished," stated Russell. "I needed to know who the different players were, what their tendencies were, their habits, and their preferences. I had to learn about their thinking, their temperaments. For me to play my best game, I had to discover theirs."

Russell epitomized what it means to be a team player. "Of all the players who ever played the game of basketball," said NBA great Bill Bradley, "Bill Russell is the first player that I would pick to start a team. He is the greatest winner in basketball history."

"The number one quality that Dwyane has as a basketball player is his ability to make everyone better. Nothing is more important to him than helping his teammates win."

—Tom Crean, Marquette University

Dwyane Wade

Today the best role model for team play in the NBA is Dwyane Wade. His driving force every day is to help his team win. In only his third year in the NBA, Dwyane led the Miami Heat to the NBA Championship.

One of Wade's role models and mentors during his years at Marquette was Bill Russell. Russell helped Wade focus more on his teammates and less on himself. The end result has been championship seasons for both Marquette and the Miami Heat. "He (Dwyane) doesn't buy into the NBA superstar hype, because he's a special kid," said former Heat teammate Damon Jones. "He's all about the team. He wants to win at all costs, and he understands he's a very integral piece of what we're doing around here. I can't even count the num-

"There's an awe about Dwyane, not only in his game but in his whole approach to life."
—Pat Riley, Miami Heat

ber of game-saving plays he has made, and never once does he boast or brag. He just goes about his work."

When Dwyane was presented the 2006 NBA Finals MVP trophy, he quickly deflected the attention from himself by saying, "This is a team award."

Wade has a gift of honesty both with himself and his teammates. What you see is what you get. In this day and age, so many people flash their agendas. His is about winning, being a good teammate, being a good husband, and being a good father. He keeps things in proper perspective and doesn't take himself too seriously.

Miami Heat coach Pat Riley is touched by Wade's genuineness. "His sincerity, his humility. All of those things are strengths when it comes to greatness," said Riley.

Former NBA player Steve Kerr concurred with Riley. "I think he's (Wade) not only a terrific player, but also a fantastic human being," said Kerr. He's a guy who will be at the forefront of the league for the

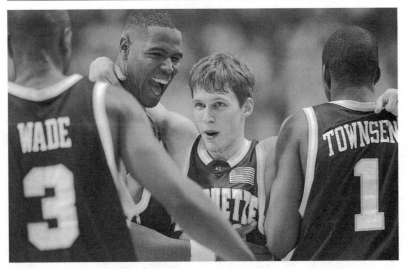

"Team chemistry translates to success on the court. We didn't have the most talented players, but we did have players that truly cared about each other."

—Travis Diener, Three-Time All-Conference USA selection

next 10 to 12 years and will be a great ambassador for the game. He's well-spoken, he's modest, yet he's confident on the floor and a leader. He's everything that our league should be about."

Esprit de Corps

The end product of teamwork and team togetherness is esprit de corps. Esprit de corps means loyalty to one's team and radiates a sense of pride, enthusiasm, and a feeling of oneness. Being on such a team creates a spirit that lives forever through the lives of the team members. It is the ultimate feeling of team togetherness and devotion to a common cause.

The United States Marine Corps motto is "Semper Fidelis," Latin for "always faithful." The Corps' values of honor, courage, and commitment are handed down from one generation of Marines to the next. And when their active duty days are over, Marines are called retired Marines or Marine veterans. There are no ex-Marines because in their culture, once a Marine, always a Marine.

One of the best examples of esprit de corps in professional basketball was the Boston Celtics during the 1950s and 1960s. The players called it Celtic Pride and described it as a culture and a practice rather than an idea. "It goes deeper than just our teams from 1956 to 1969," said team captain Bill Russell. "In fact it is totally independent of any specific year's team. It is a legacy. A passion. I am far prouder of being captain of the Boston Celtics than anything else in my career. Once you've embraced Celtic Pride, you'll never be the same."

Team pride connects the past to the present. Players from all generations are part of one team. Help your players appreciate the efforts of those that wore the uniform before them, and provide the best experience possible so they pass the torch to those that follow.

The coaches at Marquette have embraced the university's storied basketball tradition. Each year they hold an all-class reunion to honor former team members. They celebrated the 50th anniversary of the 1952 National Catholic Collegiate Championship in December 2002 with former coach Tex Winter returning for the gala event along with 18 of the original team members.

Former head coach Hank Raymonds, who won more than 71 percent of his games and led all six of his Marquette teams to post-season play, was honored prior to a game against St. Louis in 2003. His 1978 squad was ranked third in that year's final United Press International poll.

In preparation for Marquette's first Big East encounter with rival Notre Dame in 2006, the players watched clips from classic Marquette–Notre Dame games from the 1970s and 1980s, including Glenn "Doc" Rivers' winning half-court shot in 1981. It is important for players to understand history, and it's also important that they have the ability to make history. This occurred in 2006 when Marquette swept Notre Dame in the same season for the first time since 1939.

The Marquette staff wholeheartedly supported the fundraising events for the Alfred E. McGuire Center. Opened in 2003, the state-of-the-art practice facility was named for Hall of Fame coach Al McGuire. McGuire led Marquette to an NCAA championship, an NIT title, and 295 victories in 13 seasons. Since McGuire's death in 2001, Marquette players have worn a circular patch with the letters AL on their uniforms as a constant reminder of the late coach. At home games before the tip-off, the image of a golden eagle crashing through a backboard precedes a short video of the team, which is spliced with

The basketball court at the Bradley Center is named the Al McGuire Court in honor of Marquette's Hall of Fame coach.

footage of McGuire and his championship season. The legacy of McGuire and his players will always be honored at Marquette.

Instant Replay

1. A player's perception of teamwork may be a far cry from reality.
2. It is the responsibility of the head coach to demand that team basketball occurs, and the best place to start is to define the term *team player*.
3. Team players place the team ahead of personal glory and don't worry about who gets the credit as long as the team is successful.
4. Unselfishness is a prerequisite for teamwork.
5. It is a fundamental truth that team players perform because they don't want to let their teammates down.

Coach's Game Plan

ACTIVITY 3.1 Encourage each team member to take this self-assessment. Give the following instructions: Read each statement below and compare your actions to the described behavior. Using the key below, circle the number that best reflects your self-evaluation.

5 Almost always
4 Most of the time
3 Sometimes
2 Seldom
1 Almost never

Player Self-Assessment

Mission Focused

I live each day devoted to the team's core values.	**5 4 3 2 1**
I am passionately committed to the team's mission.	**5 4 3 2 1**
I always put the team's goals first.	**5 4 3 2 1**
I focus daily actions on helping the team reach its goals.	**5 4 3 2 1**
I understand the role of each team member in the mission.	**5 4 3 2 1**
I maintain focus and concentrate on the task at hand.	**5 4 3 2 1**

Unselfish

I place team victories higher than individual goals.	**5 4 3 2 1**
I am first to help teammates, last to expect special treatment.	**5 4 3 2 1**
I place the team ahead of personal glory.	**5 4 3 2 1**
I am not jealous of the success of team members.	**5 4 3 2 1**

Competitive

I bring an unquenchable desire to succeed every day.	**5 4 3 2 1**
I compete every minute on the court.	**5 4 3 2 1**
I exhibit an all-out effort 100 percent of the time.	**5 4 3 2 1**
I am first to dive for a loose ball, last to avoid physical contact.	**5 4 3 2 1**
I bring passion and high energy to the gym every day.	**5 4 3 2 1**
I am first to seek out the best competition, last to shy away.	**5 4 3 2 1**

Spirited (Will to Win)

I am first to commit, last to give less than a full effort.	**5 4 3 2 1**
I never quit.	**5 4 3 2 1**
I start and finish all endeavors with enthusiasm.	**5 4 3 2 1**

I display mental and physical toughness at all times. **5 4 3 2 1**
I stay poised under pressure. **5 4 3 2 1**
I never leave a teammate who needs help. **5 4 3 2 1**

Respectful and Trustworthy

I do not lie, cheat, steal, or intentionally deceive
    others. **5 4 3 2 1**
I am first to show concern for team members,
    last to gossip. **5 4 3 2 1**
I accept differences among team members. **5 4 3 2 1**
I listen attentively by maintaining eye contact
    with the speaker. **5 4 3 2 1**
I say "please" and "thank you." **5 4 3 2 1**

Dependable

I do what I say I will do (actions match words). **5 4 3 2 1**
I arrive early for practices, classes, and meetings. **5 4 3 2 1**
I demonstrate a positive attitude and
    am industrious. **5 4 3 2 1**
I am first to help teammates, last to criticize. **5 4 3 2 1**
I am at the right place, at the right time. **5 4 3 2 1**

Perseverance

I recover quickly from mistakes. **5 4 3 2 1**
I maintain self-confidence during difficult times. **5 4 3 2 1**
I create opportunities when obstacles get in the way. **5 4 3 2 1**

Optimistic

I am first to focus on the positive, last to dwell on
    the negative. **5 4 3 2 1**
I expect the best in times of uncertainty. **5 4 3 2 1**
I take constructive correction as a compliment. **5 4 3 2 1**

Responsible

I live according to the team's core values. **5 4 3 2 1**
I am first to accept responsibility, last to
    make excuses. **5 4 3 2 1**
I attempt to exceed standards rather than do
    the minimum. **5 4 3 2 1**

I am first to confront team violations, last to look the other way.	**5 4 3 2 1**
I turn in school assignments on time.	**5 4 3 2 1**
I do the right thing even when no one is watching.	**5 4 3 2 1**
I accept my role and fulfill it to the best of my ability.	**5 4 3 2 1**

Team Focused

I attempt to make every teammate a better player.	**5 4 3 2 1**
I am first to compliment teammates, last to discourage.	**5 4 3 2 1**
I accept and embrace discipline for the good of the team.	**5 4 3 2 1**
I am first to praise others, last to draw attention to myself.	**5 4 3 2 1**
I exemplify team pride on and off the court.	**5 4 3 2 1**
I am first to defend the team, last to criticize.	**5 4 3 2 1**
I do not allow cliques to form on the team.	**5 4 3 2 1**
I am first to lead by example, last to violate team standards.	**5 4 3 2 1**

ACTIVITY 3.2 Have your players study the results from Activity 3.1. They should select two behaviors that need improvement and then write a specific goal for each behavior and design an action plan to reach each goal.

2

Blueprint for Team Play

Being a winner in basketball comes down to three things: conditioning, fundamentals, and teamwork.

—Bill Sharman, Naismith Basketball Hall of Fame Player and Coach

Championships are won when players sacrifice personal glory for the welfare of the team.

4
Lead from the Front

The strength of any organization is a direct result of its leaders. Weak leaders equal weak organizations. Strong leaders equal strong organizations. Everything rises and falls on leadership.

—John Maxwell, Author

The transformation of a group of individuals into a united team does not happen automatically. It takes skilled leaders to convince highly talented individuals to shift their focus from themselves to the team. "Leadership is absolutely critical in our society today," said Bill Cords, athletic director at Marquette University. "We have a lot of managers but very few leaders. What we need is more leaders at

"In order for the power of teamwork to take place, the team members must share a common objective, one that is important enough to them that they are willing to make sacrifices in order to achieve it."

—Ralph Pim, United States Military Academy

every level who understand the importance of discipline, loyalty, respect, hard work, and team play."

Winning coaches are leaders who communicate their vision so others want to follow, want to be part of it, and want to make it a reality. These coaches create a group culture where players believe that giving to the team will help them be successful both individually and as a unit.

Before we discuss the characteristics of an effective coach, it is essential that we start by clarifying the reality of the coaching profession. It is a line of work that is demanding and difficult, and it provides little or no job security. Coaches must understand and accept this fact. A person considering the coaching profession should ask the question, "Why do I want to coach?" Activity 4.1 in the Coach's Game

Plan at the end of this chapter is designed to help individuals determine whether the basketball profession is the right one for them.

Coaching a team is sometimes like trying to hold a cloud in your hands. It is constantly changing shape. Bits and pieces escape. And you have to change along with it, adjusting to each new form.

—Tara VanDerveer, Women's Basketball Hall of Fame Coach

Advice for Young Coaches

First and foremost, a coach should have an unyielding passion for the game of basketball and for the players that play the game. Second, a coach should learn the profession the right way. This means learning how to teach, how to prepare, and how to compete. It is important to find mentors that will assist you in these areas. Third, coaches should always ask questions. Never become satisfied in your quest for knowledge.

No man will make a great leader who wants to do it all himself or get all the credit for doing it.

—Andrew Carnegie, Industrialist

Jason Rabedeaux, assistant coach at Marquette, urges young coaches to be passionate, patient, and loyal. Do not rush into being a head coach too soon. Find a great mentor and become a student of the game. Read the book *Make the Big Time Where You Are* by Frosty Westering. Coach Westering, legendary football coach at Pacific Lutheran University, does an outstanding job of helping young coaches discover what the "big time" really is and where it can be found in their lives.

"As a coach you must be reliable and trustworthy and expect the same from everyone else in your program."

—Tom Crean, Marquette University

Characteristics of an Effective Coach

Great coaches identify opportunities for success and empower players to win. Coaches come in all sizes and shapes, but we believe effective coaches have the following common characteristics.

Be Trustworthy

Integrity underlies everything that is done in the coaching profession. It is the foundation of how you act as a human being, a coach, and a member of society. It builds trust between you and your players. A lapse in integrity will destroy team unity.

Be Passionate

Nothing can take the place of passion in a leader's life. When leaders are passionate, it generates enthusiasm. We adhere to writer Ralph Waldo Emerson's belief that "nothing great was ever achieved with-

"Marquette basketball is all about energy and passion."

—Derek Deprey, Coordinator of Basketball Operations, Marquette University

out enthusiasm." Enthusiasm is paramount for success. A team can never reach its full potential without passion and enthusiasm.

Be Knowledgeable and Competent

Coaches should be students of the game and learn everything they can about how to do their job well. This includes understanding the laws of learning, the keys to team building, the power of positive thinking, and the importance of being technically and tactically proficient. Players look to their coaches for answers and solutions, and successful coaches produce positive results.

Be a Team Builder

Effective leaders create a work culture that promotes team play and collective responsibility. A common attribute of Hall of Fame basketball coaches is their ability to unite players and create smooth-functioning teams. John Wooden told his players, "When you come to practice, you cease to exist as an individual. You're part of a team."

Demonstrate Personal Courage and Mental Toughness

Successful leaders make courageous decisions. "The ultimate measure of a man is not where he stands in moments of comfort and convenience," stated Martin Luther King Jr., "but where he stands at times of challenge and controversy."

Through the years, many coaches have displayed courage and mental toughness by standing up for what they believed was right, regardless of the consequences. They held on to their strong convictions and beliefs with fierce determination.

Hall of Fame coach Clair Bee, who established a national power at Long Island University (LIU), was a pioneer in equality and civil rights. William "Dolly" King played for Bee at LIU from 1937 to 1941 and was later the first black player in the National Basketball League (NBL), a forerunner of today's NBA. When LIU played at Marshall University, King was told he couldn't eat with the team in the hotel's dining room. Coach Bee immediately marched his entire team into the kitchen, sat everybody down, and would not leave until every player was fed. He would not tolerate unfair treatment due to race or religion. In 2003, co-author Tom Crean was honored to be the recipient of the Clair Bee Award from the Naismith Memorial Basketball Hall of Fame.

Be a Communicator

The ability to communicate is probably the most important skill that a coach can possess, and it consists in many forms: speaking, listening, reading, and writing. Never underestimate the power of communication. You may possess great knowledge of the technical aspects of basketball, but if you cannot communicate effectively with your players and coaches, your understanding of the game is of little value. Remember that communication is not what you say, as much as what your players hear you say. Make sure that your team comprehends your intended message.

A key component of communication is active listening. It is important for coaches to realize that there is a difference between hearing and listening. "Most players only hear," said Coach Bob Knight. "The key is listening to what you're being told, what's being said, what is expected of you in your role as part of a team."

Great leaders allow others to express themselves. One of the best attributes of legendary Boston Celtics coach Red Auerbach was his ability to listen. He insisted that his players tell him exactly what was on their minds. "When I think of Red Auerbach and the leadership he provided, I think of someone who not only had a supreme bas-

"Communication is not what you say as much as what your players hear you say."

—Ralph Pim, United States Military Academy

ketball mind, but a great set of ears," said Bill Russell, who played 13 seasons for Auerbach. "Red's greatest talent was that he was a listener who translated what he heard into effective action."

Nonverbal messages are an essential component of communication in the coaching process. Coaches must be aware of such nonverbal communicators as facial expressions, eye contact, gestures, and posture. Many times, players are not comfortable speaking openly with the head coach. They pick their words carefully and do not express their true feelings. Effective coaches watch players carefully and learn to read their body language.

Be a Teacher and Motivator

The best coaches are exceptional teachers and motivators. They define, model, shape, and reinforce team play every day. Unselfish teams evolve over time through careful planning and nurturing.

"Knowledge alone is not enough to get desired results," said John Wooden. "You must have the more elusive ability to teach and to motivate. This defines a leader; if you can't teach and you can't motivate, you can't lead."

Teaching is a skill and can be improved. Be committed to becoming a master teacher and helping players develop their skills.

Be Compassionate

Successful coaches demonstrate personal concern for, and interest in, the people that work for them. Never underestimate the positive effects that compassion has on your team. Remember: People don't care how much you know, until they know how much you care.

"If you are going to coach with intensity and energy, your players must know that you love and care about them," said ESPN analyst Fran Fraschilla. "You must understand what makes your student-athletes tick, what motivates them, what irritates them, and what buttons you need to press in order to get the most out of them every day. They are not robots. They are all different."

Be Competitive

Outstanding leaders are committed to excellence and never accept anything less than the best effort. They are intensely competitive and are not afraid to take risks.

Coach Pat Summitt said, "It's my experience that people rise to the level of their own expectations and of the competition they seek out. Only by learning to compete can you discover just how much you are capable of achieving. Competitiveness is what separates achievers from the average. Too many people elect to be average, out of timidity. They are afraid to make a mistake, or to fail, or to be wrong. They are afraid to find out what's inside of them."

Focus on the Most Important Tasks

Successful coaches have the ability to focus on what's important and do not get distracted by lesser issues. College football coach Lou Holtz used the acronym WIN (What's Important Now) to illustrate this point. Weak leaders spend too much time consumed with jobs that are not essential.

In the Army, this principle is accomplished by completing a Mission Essential Task List. This list identifies tasks that are the most

"Success is not just about working hard. It is about competing every day in every thing that you do."

—Tom Crean, Marquette University

important in accomplishing the mission. It helps team members prioritize their work since there is only so much time in every day. *Army Field Manual 25–101* clearly states, "Do essential things first. . . . Nonessentials should not take up time required for essentials."

Be a Guardian of the Game

The National Association of Basketball Coaches established 12 principles in their Code of Ethics for coaches. This code is intended to serve as a guide for coaches in maintaining the highest professional level of conduct.

1. Coaches are accountable to the highest standard of honesty and integrity. All practices should be consistent with the rules of the game and the educational purposes of the institution.
2. Coaches are responsible for assisting athletes in acquiring the necessary knowledge and skills of basketball as well as promoting desirable personal and social traits in athletes under their direction.
3. Coaches treat all persons with dignity and respect, providing a model of fair play and sportsmanship.
4. Coaches observe the letter and intent of the rules of the sport and insist that athletes and teams under their direction do the same.
5. Coaches clarify in advance and act in full accordance with institutional, conference, and national governing body rules while avoiding actions that may violate the legal and/or civil rights of others.
6. Coaches have a primary concern for the health, safety, and personal welfare of each athlete. The athlete's education is also held foremost.
7. Coaches perform their duties on the basis of careful preparation, ensuring that their instruction is current and accurate. They use practices for which they are qualified and continually acquire new knowledge and skills.
8. Coaches accurately represent the competence, training, and experience of themselves and their colleagues.
9. Coaches honor all professional relationships with athletes, colleagues, officials, media, and the public. They avoid conflicts of interest and exploitation of those relationships, especially by outside parties.
10. Coaches have an obligation to respect the confidentiality of information obtained from persons in the course of their work.
11. Coaches take an active role in the prevention and treatment of drug, alcohol, and tobacco abuse.
12. Coaches carry out all obligations of employment contracts, unless released from those obligations by mutual agreement. When considering interruption or termination of service, appropriate notice is given.

Know Yourself and Seek Self-Improvement

The first Army Leadership Principle is "Know yourself and seek self-improvement." This principle should serve as a guide for all coaches because successful leaders take time to study themselves. They identify their strengths and weaknesses and continually try to improve. They lead according to their personality and do not try to copy or imitate others. Activities 4.2, 4.3, and 4.4 at the end of this chapter are designed to help coaches better understand their strengths and weaknesses.

Learn from the Legends

Make the time to study coaching legends and read carefully their words. There is so much to learn from those that have walked before us. Their experiences reveal wisdom and benchmarks for building successful teams and also serve as a source of inspiration.

An important lesson regarding a coach's responsibility to his or her players comes from Woody Hayes, the legendary football coach at Ohio State. Hayes said, "There are four ways in which I can cheat a football player. First, to do for him what he can do for himself, and thereby reduce his initiative and ingenuity. Second, by allowing him to get along on less than his best effort either in football or in the classroom. Third, by allowing him to believe that football success is all the education that he needs. And fourth, by allowing him to believe his football success makes him a privileged person."

> *Leadership is the capacity and will to rally men and women to a common purpose and the character which inspires confidence.*
>
> —Bernard Montgomery, British Field Marshal

Value-Based Coaching

We believe the game of basketball is the perfect venue to instill values and teach lessons that impact people's lives. Coaches must lead from the front to help their players reach their full potential both on and off the basketball court.

Instant Replay

1. The strength of any basketball program is the strength of its leaders.
2. Integrity underlies everything that is done in the coaching profession.
3. The coaching profession is a line of work that is demanding and difficult, and it provides little or no job security.
4. Great coaches identify opportunities for success and empower players to win.
5. Coaches must maintain the highest level of ethical conduct.

Coach's Game Plan

ACTIVITY 4.1 Is the coaching profession the right fit for you? Answer the following questions. Include specific examples to support your opinion.

1. Why do you want to coach? Explain the driving force for wanting to be in the coaching profession.
2. Are you willing to dedicate yourself 24 hours a day, seven days a week, if necessary, for your players and fellow coaches?
3. Is your family willing to bear the sacrifices?
4. Are you willing to lead by example in everything that you do? This will require you to live your life in a "fishbowl" with your professional and personal life always open to view.
5. Do you have the personal courage to live by your core values and make tough decisions regardless of the consequences?
6. Are you passionate about teaching and dedicated to helping others improve their lives?
7. Do you possess the knowledge, energy, and tenacity to lead your program to excellence?

8. Are you willing to take full responsibility for everything that happens, or doesn't happen, in your program?
9. Do you understand that loyalty is a two-way street?
10. Are you entering this profession fully understanding the risks in coaching and knowing that you may be relieved of your job at any time?

ACTIVITY 4.2 Compile a list of the factors you believe are important to become a great coach. Think about the qualities and characteristics of those coaches who have had a positive impact on your life.

ACTIVITY 4.3 List your strengths and weaknesses as a coach. Determine how you can improve your weak areas and make full use of your strengths.

ACTIVITY 4.4 Share the results of Activity 4.3 with a trusted friend or mentor. Listen carefully to his or her comments.

5
Build Your Program on Core Values

A successful man is one who can lay a firm foundation with the bricks others have thrown at him.

—David Brinkley, Television Journalist

Coaches of significance build their basketball programs on core values. Values are the heart and soul of a team and become the indispensable and lasting tenets of a program. They serve as the foundation for team play. NBA coach Pat Riley refers to a team's values as its core covenant and strongly believes all team members must endorse and uphold the covenant for the team to be successful.

"What I have learned as a head coach is that there are certain values that a player must have to be successful in our program and we must never deviate from these values."

—Tom Crean, Marquette University

In 1981, the Los Angeles Lakers were bound by a harmful core covenant. The players felt it was acceptable to put the team second whenever they felt wronged. The tension and animosity among team members grew into a cancer-like disease that eventually killed the spirit of the team.

The following year, the Lakers named Riley as their head coach. At Riley's opening team meeting, he wrote on the board: "A house divided against itself cannot stand. You are either with me or you are against me." Riley made it clear that selfishness was not acceptable and created a core covenant based on cooperation, love, hard work, and total concentration on the good of the team.

All successful organizations have shared values. The U.S. Army identifies its values with the acronym LDRSHIP, which stands for loyalty, duty, respect, selfless service, honor, integrity, and personal courage. These values apply to every soldier in every situation and are not negotiable. To serve as a constant reminder of the Army values, soldiers are issued tags imprinted with the seven values as part of their official uniform.

At Duke, Coach Mike Krzyzewski identified trust, collective responsibility, caring, communication, and pride as their core values. He compared each of these qualities to a finger on a hand. Any one individually is important. But for the hand to be powerful, all five fingers must come together and form a fist. Similarly, a group of individuals will not become a strong team until any combination of five players can play as one.

Define Your Core Values

Core values become a team's code of behavior. They define what is and what isn't acceptable. The ultimate goal is for every player to demonstrate exemplary behavior in all the team's core values. Successful coaches bridge the gap between words and action by describing the expected behavior for each core value. They set a standard and hold players accountable to this standard. Activities 5.1 and 5.2, located in the Coach's Game Plan section at the end of this chapter, are designed to help coaches identify unacceptable behaviors for team play.

The core values of Marquette basketball are integrity, respect, responsibility, unselfishness, loyalty, and tenacity. Each value is defined, and players are provided behavioral expectations for each of the values.

One of the favorite chants of the Marquette faithful is "We are Marquette." These words reverberate off the walls of the Bradley Center when the Golden Eagles are on a run. The coaching staff added three words to the chant and placed them on a sign located in the hallway close to the entrance of the coaches' offices. It symbolizes Marquette basketball. The sign reads "We Are Toughness, We Are Marquette."

"The qualities of Marquette basketball become instilled in each of us as players . . . and eventually, a player begins living out these principles every day in everything he does both on and off the court."

—Travis Diener, Three-Time All-Conference USA selection

Integrity

Integrity is the cornerstone of good character and encompasses every part of your life. If you have integrity, your words are free from deceit and your actions are consistent with your words. You know what you stand for, and you live by the standards that you set. Integrity demands that we pay our debts on time, return items that someone else has lost, and follow rules and regulations.

A player with integrity:

1. Does not lie, cheat, or steal
2. Is always honest with himself or herself
3. Does not intentionally deceive others
4. Is a person of his or her word

Respect

Respect is treating people the way they should be treated. If you are respectful, you recognize the dignity and worth of all individuals and honor their beliefs, customs, and heritage. Respect is an essential

"The coaching staff embraced me as one of their own and taught me so many things. Things like how to talk with people, how to look them in their eyes when you talk with them, and how to show them respect."

—Joe Chapman, Marquette University letter winner 2003–06

component of an effective team and is demonstrated by having a genuine concern for the safety and well-being of others.

In Marquette's locker room there is a sign that describes the expectations for each player. It reads:

1. Give eye contact.
2. Say "please" and "thank you."
3. Be on time.
4. Pay attention.
5. Don't let your teammates fail.

A player with respect:

1. Accepts the differences among team members
2. Listens attentively and gives eye contact to the speaker
3. Takes constructive criticism from coaches as a compliment
4. Says "please" and "thank you"
5. Shows consideration for others, including opponents and officials

"Always have the mentality that there is someone out there working harder than you. You can never stop pushing yourself to get better."

—Todd Townsend,
Marquette University letter winner 2002–05

Responsibility

When you are responsible, you are dependable and reliable and all team members can count on you. You work hard to improve and have the perseverance to get through difficult times. You are committed to excellence and do everything within your power to complete the mission of the team.

A player with responsibility:

1. Adheres to the rules and regulations of the university and the team
2. Does the right thing even when no one is watching
3. Leads by example
4. Strives to be the best both on and off the court
5. Is at the right place, at the right time

Unselfishness

Unselfishness or selfless service is putting the needs of the team ahead of your own. It is taking every action possible to provide for the wel-

"The first player that I think of as a team player is Travis Diener. He is totally unselfish. He knows what he has to do in order to make everyone around him a better player."

—Steve Novak, 2006 First Team All-Big East Conference selection

fare of your team members. You demonstrate unselfishness by accepting the role that makes the team stronger and speaking supportively of all team members.

An unselfish player:

1. Sacrifices personal glory for the welfare of the team
2. Helps others succeed both on and off the court
3. Plays his or her role to the fullest
4. Is not jealous of the success of teammates

Loyalty

Loyalty is the most important resource of a team and must be a two-way street. Not only should players be loyal to their coach, coaches should be loyal to their players. Players demonstrate loyalty by supporting the decisions of coaches, standing up for teammates, and adhering to the program's core values. Coaches demonstrate loyalty by providing their players the maximum opportunity for personal and professional growth and by protecting them against unfair treatment.

"Our team unity and loyalty to each other is a year-round thing. It doesn't stop at the end of the basketball season."

—Marcus Jackson,
Marquette University letter winner 2004–05

A player with loyalty:

1. Adheres to the core values of the program
2. Is devoted to the team's vision and mission
3. Demonstrates faithfulness and truthfulness to all team members
4. Confronts team violators and does not look the other way

Tenacity

Tenacity is the trademark of Marquette basketball and refers to the mental and physical toughness of every team member. When you are tenacious, you dive for loose balls and take charges. Tenacious play-

"It was a war for some of those drills, crashing and diving. You would see bodies flying. When you see that in practices, you would not be surprised to see it in games."

—Lori Nickel, sportswriter, *Milwaukee Journal Sentinel*

ers relish competition and do not shy away from physical contact. They take pride in knowing an opponent will never outwork them.

A trademark of every player who has successfully completed our program is they will never quit. This one component separates great players from good players. Great players are relentless in the pursuit of their dreams. They overcome challenges and disappointments. They persevere and keep fighting regardless of the conditions.

A great way to measure tenacity is by watching players during the course of a 40-minute game. Does the score or the amount of time left in a game affect the players' attitudes and intensity levels? Tenacious players are warriors. They make the maximum effort, every minute of every game. A spectator walking into the arena should not be able to tell from the intensity level whether it is a 1-point game or a 20-point game.

"There was no 'out of bounds' in the Marquette practices. The players went after a loose ball until someone came up with it."

—John Baker, photographer for the Marquette University basketball website

Quitting is not an option. Even when the outcome of a game has been decided, players must play hard until the game is over. As coaches, we never stop coaching. Our teams are always trying to make one more basket or get one more defensive stop.

The Marquette game at the University of North Carolina on January 13, 2001, illustrates the importance of never giving up. The Golden Eagles lost the nationally televised game 84–54, but it was not an embarrassing loss. Marquette players fought hard until the end. It was a valuable experience because the players learned how far they had to go in order to be one of the best teams in the country, and they began to understand the importance of playing hard for 40 minutes, no matter what the score. ABC's Brad Nessler acknowledged Marquette's intensity during the broadcast. "There'll be brighter times, because you can't play as hard as they have (Marquette) played and have the fruits of your efforts go unrewarded," Nessler said.

A player with tenacity:

1. Competes every second on the court
2. Perseveres through difficult times
3. Never quits
4. Brings positive energy to the team every day

What Are the Core Values of Your Team?

Ask yourself, "What does my basketball program stand for?" Read the list of values and qualities below to see which ones fit best into your philosophy. Be sure to complete Activities 5.3 and 5.4 in the Coach's Game Plan at the end of this chapter.

Values and Qualities of Teams

aggressiveness	anticipation	assertiveness	balance	commitment
compassion	competence	competitive	concentration	confidence
consistency	conviction	cooperation	courage	curiosity
dependability	desire	determination	devotion	discipline
drive	duty	energy	enthusiasm	excellence
faith	fearlessness	flexibility	fortitude	giving
gratitude	heart	honesty	honor	humility
humor	industriousness	initiative	inspiration	integrity
intensity	imagination	loyalty	optimism	passion
patience	perseverance	persistence	poise	positive attitude
pride	preparedness	punctuality	reliability	resolve
resourcefulness	respect	responsibility	risk-taking	self-control
selfless service	sharing	spirit	teamwork	tenacity
timeliness	trust	truth	unity	vigor
vision	vitality			

Keep Your Core Values at the Forefront

Core values are the guiding principles for everything that is done within a program. Effective leaders find ways to keep their core values at the forefront at all times. One way is to use acronyms. If the core values of a team are discipline, integrity, respect, and toughness, the acronym DIRT could be used to reinforce the blue-collar work ethic. It symbolizes the importance of getting your hands dirty in order to complete a task. The acronym COMPETE could be used to establish the trademark of competitiveness. The letters stand for consistency, ownership, mastery, persistence, energy, toughness, and enthusiasm.

> *Our mission statement, our strategic plan, and our entire approach at North Carolina were to play hard, play smart, and play together.*
>
> —Dean Smith, Naismith Basketball Hall of Fame Coach

Another way to communicate your core values is to use short phrases that accentuate the expected behavior of team members. An example in the Army is The Soldier's Creed. Derived from the seven Army Values, the Creed describes the behavioral expectation for soldiers. The Soldier's Creed includes:

- I will always place the mission first.
- I will never accept defeat.
- I will never quit.
- I will never leave a fallen comrade.

Team Ownership of the Core Values

Championship teams have players that embrace and take ownership of the team's core values. They understand that it is the responsibility of all team members to make sure that everyone adheres to these principles. Any slippage in this area results in cracks in the foundation of the program. Unless these cracks are repaired immediately, internal dissension will keep the team from reaching its full potential.

At West Point, the Department of Physical Education's motto is "Set the Standard; Maintain the Standard." It simply means there are behavioral expectations for all team members and it is the responsibility of each person to make sure the standards are met. If someone is not meeting the standard, he or she is to be confronted by a teammate.

There are only two choices when it comes to team values. A player is either fully committed or selectively picks the time to be committed. Winning teams have players that are fully committed.

Positive Peer Pressure

One of the best ways to change the behavior of uncommitted teammates is through positive peer pressure. Pat Riley led the Los Angeles Lakers to four NBA championships during the 1980s. On the way to winning the 1982 NBA title, Riley told his players, "You as a team have set standards that you think will make us a championship team. We as a group will monitor each other. And I as your coach will enforce them."

Ted Johnson, a member of three NFL championship teams while playing for New England, believed that part of the Patriots' success was due to peer pressure. "There's a company culture, there's an expectation of winning," said Johnson. "It's not only expected from our coaching staff and management, but from the players that are here year in and year out. On this team, there's a tremendous amount of peer pressure to play to your ability and to work hard and to buy into the system. That, to me, is what makes it work."

Players on Marquette's Final Four team in 2003 held each other accountable for adherence to the team's principles. Teammates did not hesitate to confront a player who violated the team's core values. In the NCAA Tournament game against Holy Cross, Dwyane Wade did not score a point in the first half. Travis Diener felt that Wade's scoring struggles were affecting his attitude, and he told Wade about it at halftime.

"I wasn't scoring, was all into myself, and Travis let me know about it," remembered Wade. "Sometimes he would speak to you in a real quiet tone; other times he would get into your face."

"Dwyane and Travis were great leaders. They had two different ways of getting it across but it was very effective. Players fall in line with the expectations that your best players have for themselves."

—Tom Crean, Marquette University

When there is respect and trust among team members, a confrontation such as this can produce positive results. In the second half against Holy Cross, Wade scored 15 points and together he and Diener delivered 14 of the final 16 points in Marquette's 4-point victory.

Don't play players only because they have potential if they do not hustle, work hard, and listen.

—Morgan Wootten, Naismith Basketball Hall of Fame Coach

Commitment from the Team's Star Player

Key players are often the coach's bridge to team leadership. Players generally fall in line with the expectations that star players have for themselves. In 1967, Wilt Chamberlain was the catalyst that helped the Philadelphia 76ers capture the NBA championship. Chamberlain was an offensive force second to none, but he had a reputation for being a one-dimensional player. Under the tutelage of Hall of Fame coach Alex Hannum, Chamberlain altered his game to one of defense, rebounding, and team play. His teammates followed his example, and the 76ers won 68 games and were later selected as the NBA's best team during the league's first 35 years.

In 1987, Michael Jordan averaged more than 37 points per game, but the Chicago Bulls won only 24 percent of their games. Under the guidance of Coach Phil Jackson, the Bulls were changed from a showcase for Jordan to a balanced, unselfish team with Jordan leading the way. Jordan's scoring dropped 20 percent but in the process, Chicago won six NBA championships.

Patience Is a Virtue

Good things take time. The culture of a team cannot be changed overnight. Successful leaders set the example by modeling their organization's core values both on and off the court. They consistently hold team members accountable for their actions. They reinforce positive behaviors and make corrections when something does not meet the standard. When the players come forward and their actions demonstrate commitment to the core values, the team is ready for its ascent.

Instant Replay

1. Build your team's foundation on core values.
2. Define your core values and establish behavioral objectives for each one.
3. Create a team covenant from your core values.
4. Great teams have players that take ownership of the team covenant.
5. It is the responsibility of all team members to make sure that everyone adheres to the core values.

Coach's Game Plan

ACTIVITY 5.1 What behaviors in your program are unacceptable and will result in a player being suspended or dismissed from your team?

ACTIVITY 5.2 What behaviors in practice are unacceptable and will result in a player being removed from that day's workout?

ACTIVITY 5.3 List the core values of your basketball program. Keep the number of core values to a minimum. Select only those that best represent your program.

ACTIVITY 5.4 Describe the behavioral expectation for each of the values listed in the previous activity. Be specific. Players must have a clear understanding of the behavior that is expected of them.

6

Begin with the End in Mind

Personal leadership is the process of keeping your vision and values before you and aligning your life to be congruent with them.

—Stephen Covey, Author

Basketball championships don't just happen. Planning is an essential component for success. Author Stephen Covey coined the phrase "begin with the end in mind" to emphasize the power of planning.

There are some areas in our lives where we do an excellent job of beginning with the end in mind. Take a vacation, for example. How many people starting a vacation would just get into their cars and drive aimlessly hoping to find the right spot? Or go to an airport and then decide their destination? No, chances are, you'd have the time planned out with the sights you want to see, the people you want to visit, hotel reservations, appropriate clothing, and the amount of money you plan to spend.

The same can be said for successful basketball coaches. They have a clear vision for their program and picture the desired result before they even begin. John Thompson began with the end in mind when he accepted the coaching position at downtrodden Georgetown University in 1972. The school had a dismal 3-23 record and was a far cry from being a basketball power. The day Thompson took over, he gathered his ragtag Georgetown team, pointed to the wall in the gym, and predicted that someday a national championship banner would hang there. In 1984, the Hoyas beat Houston in the NCAA Finals, and the national championship Thompson had predicted came to Georgetown.

Blue-Sky Thinking

There is one universal rule of planning: You will never be bigger than the vision that guides you. Marquette coaching legend Al McGuire expressed this concept with the following advice: "Dream big. Don't be just another guy going down the street going nowhere."

Use your imagination to visualize the desired end state for your program. When people free their imaginations, they begin to see limitless horizons. Pat Williams, senior vice-president of the Orlando Magic, calls this blue-sky thinking.

The players at Marquette were introduced to the concept of blue-sky thinking at our first team meeting that took place in March 1999. They were told that Marquette basketball would regain national prominence and showcase the most tenacious team in the country. A nere four years later, the Golden Eagles returned to the Final Four for the first time since 1977 because the players followed a blueprint of mental and physical toughness, integrity, optimism, and unselfishness.

Cherish your vision and your dreams as they are the children of your soul; the blueprints of your ultimate achievements.

—Napoleon Hill, author of *Think and Grow Rich*, one of the all-time bestselling books in the field of motivation

Shared Vision

A great coach is a servant for his or her dream and understands the genesis of the dream is unimportant. The key factor is whether the team members take ownership of the vision. For true success to occur, all players must be united and committed to the dream.

"You must get the players to believe that your vision will help them be successful both individually and as a unit," said Fran Fraschilla. "Any successful team has its own culture of success. It definitely starts with the head coach, permeates down through the assistant coaches, managers, the rest of the staff, and then the players. The culture establishes a road map for success. It encompasses a vision and what the end result will look like."

Visions are never the sole property of one man or one woman. Before a vision can become reality, it must be owned by every single member of the group.

—Phil Jackson, NBA Championship Coach

Put Your Vision in Writing

Do you want to pave the way to success and get your players headed toward the same goal? Then put your vision in a written statement that is clearly understood by all your players. A vision statement helps you stay on course and corrects you when you stray. It makes team members feel proud and excited to be part of something bigger than themselves. It also requires players to stretch their expectations, aspirations, and performances.

Vision statements are not wishful thinking. They are based on the reality of your resources and talent. Pat Riley believes that great coaches define reality but also show their players what reality could and should be. An example of a national leader that demonstrated this belief was Martin Luther King Jr. King was a dominant force in the civil rights movement because he didn't accept the world as it was and showed people the way it should be.

> *All our dreams can come true, if we have the courage*
> *to pursue them.*
>
> —Walt Disney, Founder of Disneyland and Walt Disney World

What is your dream for your basketball program? Is it written in a vision statement? If not, you will have an opportunity to create a vision statement in Activity 6.1 at the end of this chapter. Here are several suggestions for writing your vision statement:

1. Assess your program's resources and the talent level of your team members. Be realistic about the current state of your program, but also consider its vast potential.
2. Identify the desired end state.
3. Involve members of your team and get their input.
4. Write the vision statement choosing words that are clear and explicit. Keep the statement relatively short so it can be easily remembered.
5. Take your vision statement to your administration and get their support.
6. Keep your program's vision visible.

Consider having your vision statement displayed on a sign in your team room, or put it inside each player's locker. The NBA Orlando Magic showcase their vision statement on a large plaque in the reception area. It clearly expresses the club's vision "to become the professional sports model of the twenty-first century through an unwavering commitment to integrity, service, quality, and consumer value" and can be easily read by anyone that enters the office.

The Power of Visual Images

Pictures and motivational signs can be used to reinforce a team's vision. At Marquette there are constant reminders everywhere, from the hallways to the locker room, the film room to the showers. The moment a player walks through the front door he sees images showing the tradition and pride of Marquette basketball.

"Initially the motivational signs are things that players look at and read," explained Travis Diener. "Then at some point, each player internalizes the meaning of the words. Eventually, a player begins living out these values in everything he does both on and off the court."

Three powerful images—the Superdome, a baseball bat, and a lunch pail—were utilized by Marquette during their Final Four season. Each played a key role in the success of the team.

The Louisiana Superdome

In 2002, the basketball staff at Marquette combined Covey's "begin with the end in mind" concept with the adage "seeing is believing" by ordering a print of the New Orleans Superdome, site of the 2003 NCAA Finals. The picture was unveiled in November after the second exhibition game because the team needed more focus. Players were told that they had to practice harder and bring their best effort to every game. Only by doing this could the team reach its full potential and go to the Final Four. Each player was then asked to make a decision. If he was going to commit 100 percent every day, he was told to sign his name on the picture of the Superdome. There was no in between. A player was either "in" or "out."

Everyone signed the picture, including coaches, players, managers, trainers, strength coach, and priest. The team's goal of reaching the Final Four became a focal point because of the image of the Superdome. It reinforced the responsibility of each player to make this happen. The picture was framed and taken everywhere—buses, planes, locker rooms, and meeting rooms. You name it and the picture was there. It even had its own seat on the team's charter plane.

Later that season when Marquette traveled to New Orleans to play Tulane University, Assistant Coach Trey Schwab, unbeknownst to the players, arranged for a tour of the Superdome. After the shoot-around at Tulane, everyone boarded the bus thinking they were headed back to the hotel. When some of the players wondered whether they were headed in the right direction, their question was quickly dismissed. As the bus pulled up in front of the Superdome, this simple but direct message was delivered to the team: "Before you can achieve it, you have to be able to see it, and now you are going to see it for real."

Walking into one of the most recognizable sporting venues in America, one could feel an aura of familiarity, a sense of purpose. All of a sudden, the reason why the team had worked so hard the entire year was in front of them. Even though there was no basketball court in place, the guide walked everyone to the exact spot where center court would be. The players and coaches gathered together and had a team picture taken. "I had never seen anything like it," said Steve Novak. "I was imagining myself playing in that place with every seat filled."

"The coaching staff wanted us to know the magnitude of their vision for our team," said Todd Townsend. "We had players such as Dwyane Wade, Robert Jackson, and Travis Diener that were the leaders of the team and knew that we could win it all. But you also had younger guys that probably initially signed the picture because it seemed like the right thing to do.

"As we took the tour of the Superdome, we began to think that this was for real. I swear to you, as the guide was giving us the tour, I actually began seeing myself playing there in the Final Four. At that moment was when I started dreaming big. I began telling myself that we could really do it. I could actually see it and feel it! This is one of those things that the coaches had planned, and it worked perfectly. For them to take us to the Superdome, it got us excited and believing that we could do this."

The Baseball Bat

During the summer of 2002, the Marquette coaches purchased a black bat at Miller Park in Milwaukee and had the words *character*, *toughness*, and *unselfishness* engraved on it. The staff didn't know exactly how or when it should be introduced to the team so the bat was temporarily put aside.

After losing two close games at East Carolina and Dayton, everyone's nerves were fragmented and tempers were short. The team was preparing to play at St. Louis, and it was decided that it was time to bring out the bat. The night before the game, the players had their normal scouting report, watched game film, and had something to eat. Then the room was darkened and the team watched a riveting film clip in *Saving Private Ryan* that emphasized the importance of the warrior ethos. The staff's message to the players was that successful teams are prepared for battle and refuse to be outfought. The bat was unveiled and raised toward the ceiling, and the players were told it was the team's "road stick." It represented Marquette's character, toughness, and unselfishness. Everyone then signed the bat with a gold pen.

"The baseball bat symbolized what Marquette basketball was all about," said Townsend. "It was another defining moment in the season. We had the Superdome picture and now the bat. From that point on, the bat was held up before every game and you could feel the excitement as we were getting ready to go into battle."

The Lunch Pail

After Marquette's shoot-around on the day of their NCAA tournament game against Missouri, Tom Zupanic, vice-president of the Indianapolis Colts, spoke to the team. He walked in, put a lunch pail in the middle of the room, and began talking about the Colts' drive to the AFC Championship game. The lunch pail represented the blue-collar mentality of their team. The Colts had players who believed in themselves when nobody else did and found a way to get to the AFC title game. It was an exhilarating message because it described perfectly the mentality of Marquette's players. The lunch pail became a symbol of Marquette's toughness and had a special spot on the team's bench against Missouri and the games that followed on the way to the Final Four.

Instant Replay

1. Successful basketball coaches have a clear vision for their program and picture the desired result before they even begin.
2. You will never be bigger than the vision that guides you.
3. Great coaches define reality but also show their players what reality could and should be.
4. Team members must take ownership of the vision for the team to be successful.
5. A vision statement should be clear, explicit, and short.

Coach's Game Plan

ACTIVITY 6.1 Write a vision statement for your basketball program.

7

Select Talented Team Players

Endeavors succeed or fail because of the people involved. Only by attracting the best people will you accomplish great deeds.

—Colin L. Powell, Former Secretary of State

You win with talented team players. The best programs in the country have highly gifted players who want to play in a team environment and coaches who do not deviate from the program's core values when selecting players for their team.

Marquette searches for talented team players who are stereotypical gym rats and come from winning programs. The coaching staff wants athletes who combine the motor skills of balance, agility, coordination, speed, power, and quickness with highly developed basketball skills. These players are also characterized by their blue-collar work ethic, love of the game, and ethical behavior. They demonstrate respect for coaches and teammates and embrace discipline for the benefit of the team. Their actions model integrity and unselfishness.

A talented player lacking character will destroy team unity and team play. Don't overestimate your ability to transform undisciplined and disobedient prospects into team players. These players require hours of individual attention and most often upset the chemistry of your team. Initially, players committed to the team's core values will try and bring these individuals into the fold. If this doesn't work, the committed players often become frustrated. Eventually their frustration can lead to questioning the leadership of the coaches for allowing undisciplined players to disrupt the effectiveness and togetherness of the team. Always go with the players who have a little less talent but more dedication and more singleness of purpose.

To be a coach is to be a teacher. You have to teach people from different backgrounds to work together for the common good.

—Nat Holman, Naismith Basketball Hall of Fame Coach

Character

The greatest challenge for coaches is to find talented players of character. It is essential that no stone is left unturned when investigating the character of prospective players. At Marquette, the core values of integrity, respect, responsibility, unselfishness, and tenacity are always at the forefront when evaluating recruits.

"Character, toughness, and unselfishness are the three defining qualities of the basketball program at Marquette," said Chris Grimm, a three-year letter winner. "Our coaches hold these qualities in high regard and will not bring in a player that doesn't fit with the rest of us."

"A player must be of high character and be mentally and physically tough to succeed at Marquette."

—Chris Grimm, Marquette University letter winner 2003–06

Learning the value of team play is to learn one of life's lessons.

—H. C. "Doc" Carlson, Naismith Basketball Hall of Fame Coach

The following sections describe some of the qualities Marquette's coaching staff considers when evaluating recruits.

Integrity

A recruit must be honest. Listen carefully to what a player says and then observe his or her actions. Make sure they are one and the same. Any breach of integrity is a showstopper. Period.

Respect

Two-way relationships create the framework for teamwork. When selecting players for your team, observe the relationships these players have with their parents, friends, teachers, teammates, coaches, opponents, and referees. If they are disrespectful to any of these people, a red flag should go up immediately because they will probably not make good team members. The first step in team-building is respect.

Dwyane Wade is an excellent example of the importance of respect. As a senior at Richards High School in Oak Lawn, Illinois, Wade was having a difficult time meeting the academic standards necessary to play Division I basketball. His positive attitude, respect for authority, and desire to succeed academically set him apart from most students. One teacher, who had been at the high school for 27 years, described Wade as one of the three finest people that had attended the school during his tenure. This teacher's recommendation played an important part in Marquette's confidence in Wade, both as a person and a student.

Wade missed the required ACT score by one point and many colleges and universities stopped recruiting him. But the coaching staff at Marquette was so impressed with Wade's moral fiber that they recommended he still be given an opportunity at Marquette. The admissions committee accepted Wade based on his strong character, and he became the first partial qualifier in school history. Their decision to give Wade an opportunity was the catalyst for where he is today.

Responsibility

A recruit should accept responsibility for his or her success academically, athletically, and socially. Players must value the importance of an education and have a thirst for knowledge. Responsible players work hard academically and do not expect favors or special treatment in the classroom.

Select players who are driven to reach their full potential. Look for prospects who have a positive attitude and high energy and who are consumed with getting better. They love being part of a team and channel their energy into learning how to play the game the right way. They want to be coached and consider criticism as a compliment because it comes from coaches who are trying to help them improve.

A great example of a player driven to reach his full potential is Marquette player Ousmane Barro. Ousmane was born and raised in Dakar, Senegal, and did not play high school basketball. Even though he demonstrated outstanding athletic potential, there were many question marks about his ability to develop the basketball skills necessary for success on the Division I level. During his freshman year, Barro was inconsistent and struggled. But he did not let that affect his positive attitude and work ethic. Ousmane continued to work on his game and made unbelievable progress during the next twelve months. In 2006, he finished second on the team in blocked shots and field goal percentage. In the NCAA Tournament game against Alabama, Ousmane scored 13 points and had three blocked shots. He has earned the respect of Marquette fans and the chant of "Ooze" can be heard throughout the Bradley Center on game night. For his hard work and dedication to improve, Ousmane was presented the 2006 Most Improved Player Award.

Even though Steve Novak was one of the best shooters in the country coming out of high school, he demonstrated an unquenchable thirst to improve. For every free throw he missed during a game, Novak would go back on the court after the game ended and shoot 50 free throws. "I don't know that necessarily cures it," Novak said. "There's no question that becoming a good free throw shooter and making them consistently is something that happens over years, but I think that doing that kind of thing is a good way of getting back on track."

During Novak's freshman year in a game at the University of North Carolina at Charlotte, he was fouled with several seconds left. Marquette was leading by two points. He made the first free throw to stretch Marquette's lead to three points, but he missed the second, which would have put the game out of reach. Fortunately, Marquette held on for its first win ever against a North Carolina team in the Tar Heel State. Novak jubilantly celebrated the win with his teammates but was inwardly disappointed because he missed the last free throw.

"I felt that I had let my teammates down," said Novak. "I received permission from the coaches to go back on the floor and shoot, but our academic advisor Denny Kuiper said that I could have only two attempts. He wanted it to be similar to game conditions. That made a lot of sense to me, so we went out and I knocked down both free throws. It was the perfect way to put closure to the fact that I had missed my final free throw."

Novak's quest for perfection paid off as he made 68 consecutive free throws in 2006 to set a new Marquette record. His personal best in practice is 212 consecutive free throws. "I definitely take pride in making them," he said. "Whenever you put time into something and care about something, it's satisfying to succeed."

Responsibility means understanding what it takes to win. Search for players who come from programs where winning is expected.

In 2006 Steve Novak made 68 consecutive free throws to set a new Marquette record.

These players understand the power of desire, persistence, and pride. They have the ability to perform at their best even when they are hurt, sick, or troubled. They always make the extra effort because they want to win.

Socially responsible players make good choices. They realize there are consequences for making bad decisions. They hold themselves accountable for their actions and do not blame others for their mistakes.

Unselfishness

Select players who exhibit a team-first attitude and are talking more about winning championships than winning individual honors. Avoid players that are critical of their teammates and think they are not being used properly by their coaches. Their air of entitlement will be a team killer.

Dan Fitzgerald is a good example of a player who is willing to do anything to help the team win. The 6'9" transfer from Tulane University was asked to guard anyone from point guards to centers during the 2006 season. After scoring 18 points in Marquette's victory over DePaul, Fitzgerald said, "I played a lot of point guard, two [big guard], three [small forward], and even the four position [power for-

"My mental toughness since coming to Marquette has gone to a level that I never thought that I would have. The life lesson that I will carry with me forever is my ability to persevere."

—Steve Novak, Second Round selection of the Houston Rockets in the 2006 NBA Draft

ward] tonight. I am willing to do whatever it takes and play wherever. We are a defensive-minded team. My job is to guard first and foremost, and this game was no different."

Look for talented players who are unselfish and have high energy. We like to refer to these players as "battery chargers" because they ignite the passion in fellow team members. Marquette's recruiting class of 2005 (Dominic James, Jamil Lott, Wesley Matthews, and Jerel McNeal) is so special because of their unselfishness and their understanding of the team concept. The newcomers respected the upperclassmen and valued their opinions. Together they bonded to form a united team.

Earvin "Magic" Johnson is a prime example of a "battery charger." Few players in basketball history have exhibited as much enthusiasm or displayed such an engaging personality both on and off the court. His trademark smile could light up an arena from coast to coast. Magic led his teams to championships at the high school, college, professional, and international levels. He was the epitome of self-lessness and could dominate a game without scoring a point. He had a guard's mentality in a forward's body. Magic could rebound, shoot, pass, post-up, and defend. He made the triple-double fashionable and changed the game as a 6′9″ guard.

"Whatever it took to win, I would do," said Johnson. "It was never about me but always about the team. I miss the camaraderie of 12 guys going to war, walking down the tunnel and knowing it is you against everybody else."

Mental and Physical Toughness

A recruit must demonstrate toughness because it is a prerequisite for team success. Toughness cannot be turned on and off like a light in a dark room. It is a talent that must be developed. Over time, it becomes a defining characteristic of a player and eventually the team.

There are two types of toughness—mental and physical. Mentally tough players stay focused and compete every minute on the court. They maintain their composure when unexpected situations occur during practices or games. They persevere through difficult times and never quit. Mentally tough players prepare to win. They get to practice early and are focused on what must be done in order to make the team better. They do not walk on the court at the last minute because they were outside the locker room saying goodbye to their friends or talking on their cell phones.

Physically tough players recognize that basketball is a contact sport where only the strong survive. They are aggressive and do not hesitate to dive for a loose ball, take a charge, or drive to the basket knowing they will probably be fouled. Joe Chapman showed Marquette's coaching staff his tenacity when he took three straight charges in a high school all-star game. Chapman became a four-year standout for Marquette and earned the Hit the Deck Award in 2006. This award is presented each year to a Marquette player for his physical play and willingness to take a charge and sacrifice his body for the team.

A tenacious player must also be highly competitive and driven to become the best player possible. Competitors know how to win. They seek out the highest level of competition. They continually set new goals and feel the need to raise the bar. Competitors know they will face players with more talent but none more competitive. They

Dwyane Wade secures a loose ball and calls
time-out before going into the crowd in the 2003
NCAA Regional Finals against Kentucky.

simply won't fail from a lack of effort, lack of commitment, or lack of determination. Anything short of their best is not enough and unacceptable.

Travis Diener is one of the most competitive people in the world today. The Marquette coaching staff knew they absolutely had to get him after seeing him play only twice. His competitive mind-set and confident demeanor clearly set him apart from other players.

"Let's face it," said Diener, "I'm a skinny, short guy playing a game for athletic, taller, stronger guys. For me to be successful, I have to outwork, outhustle, outplay people. I have to outthink them. That's what I've done my whole life. I don't think anyone plays with more heart than I do."

Have Prospects Watch Practice

The best way to understand Marquette basketball is to watch practice. We want recruits to see the level of intensity required for them to play in Marquette's program. In just one day, prospects will gain an appreciation for the mental and physical toughness required for success. If they are not committed to hard work, it is best to know from the very beginning and allow them to choose another path.

Marquette's emphasis on toughness and intensity is apparent the moment someone walks into a practice. Many times, the rules are altered and the out-of-bounds lines are ignored. Players are expected to go after a loose ball until someone comes up with it. The contact between players makes the scrimmage look more like hockey than basketball.

"They (practices) are very intense, almost brutal," said Todd Rosniak of the *Milwaukee Journal Sentinel*. "The practices are so defensive-oriented, so hustle-oriented, so toughness-oriented. All 10 players are expected to go after the ball. Three or four guys would dive into doors or the bleachers. It was like a free-for-all scrum on the floor. The entire team would form a circle around the players, cheering on the guys going for the ball."

New York Daily News basketball writer Dick "Hoops" Weiss watched Marquette's practice prior to their game with Louisville in 2003 and said, "It was the most physically intense workout I have witnessed and goes a long way to explain why Marquette plays as hard as any team in the country."

It is the belief of Marquette coaches that athletes today are still looking for discipline. They want to play for coaches who will help them reach their potential. They want someone to believe in them, to teach them, and to lead them. They also want to surround themselves with teammates who have the same work ethic and who are passionate about winning championships.

Motor Skills

A prerequisite when selecting players for your team is versatility. Players must have the physical attributes that allow them to be successful on both ends of the court. Jerel McNeal is the epitome of versatility. He can score on the break or in the half court. He's an outstanding driver, rebounds with energy, and plays with pure heart. His ability to score is overshadowed by his unselfish defense.

Balance, agility, coordination, speed, power, and quickness are critical motor skills for a basketball player. There is no substitute for quickness. John Wooden regarded quickness under control as one of the most important attributes of a player. "Be quick—but don't hurry" was one of Wooden's favorite expressions because he believed basketball must be played fast but never out of control.

To identify strengths and weaknesses of basketball players, Scott Holsopple, head strength and conditioning coach at Marquette, utilizes an assessment similar to the one used by the NBA during their Pre-Draft Camp in Chicago. The test items are body measurements, speed/agility measurements, explosive measurements.

Body Measurements

The four important body measurements when assessing basketball players are height, weight, wingspan, and standing reach.

HEIGHT. Height is the distance from the top of the head to the soles of the feet. To measure, have the player remove shoes and stand with heels and upper back against a wall. A coach brings the measuring instrument down until it touches the top of the head and is level. When the player steps away from the wall, height is determined by the placement of the measuring instrument.

WEIGHT. Weight is the sum of body fat and lean body mass. Players should always remove shoes. Then they step onto the scale, making sure all parts of their feet are on the platform. Make sure the scale is set to zero. Wait for the scale to display the weight, or move the sliding arrow till the scale balances parallel to the floor.

WINGSPAN. The wingspan is the horizontal measurement of outstretched arms from one hand to the other. The measurement of a player's wingspan is more important than height in evaluating talent. Dwyane Wade stands 6′4″ but has the wingspan of a player 6′11″. To measure wingspan, a ruler or tape measure is displayed horizontally on the wall at shoulder height. The player stands facing the wall and sets the tip of the middle finger at one end of the measuring instrument, stretching the body flat against the wall to reach to place the other middle finger as far to the other end of the measuring instrument as possible. Record the longest measure the arms can reach.

STANDING REACH. The standing reach is the measure of total height from the soles of the feet to the top of the fingers with arms stretched overhead. A ruler or tape measure is displayed vertically on the wall. Players stand facing the wall. They place one hand over the other, stacking fingers. With toes touching the wall and feet flat on the ground, they reach stacked hands as high as possible. Record the highest point that the fingers can touch.

Speed/Agility Measurements

Speed can be defined as the ability to cover a given distance in the shortest amount of time. Maximal attainable speed is dependent on the direction of movement (i.e., forward, backward, laterally, and so on). *Agility* is the ability of an athlete to change direction while maintaining speed and balance.

BOX DRILL. This box drill measures a player's ability to change direction forward, backward, and sideways in a quick and efficient manner. Begin at the top left-hand corner of the paint area (NBA basketball court dimensions, 17-foot width). Players should sprint to the baseline, then slide without crossing feet to the corner of the box,

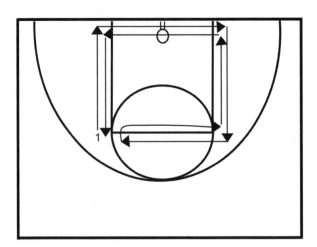

backpedal to the free throw line, and slide to the opposite end of the line. Immediately they return by sliding to the opposite corner of the free throw line, sprinting to the baseline, sliding to the opposite corner of the box, and backpedaling to finish at the free throw line. The athlete always faces the baseline and never crosses his or her feet when sliding. If using a hand timer, repeat three times and take the average time.

¾-COURT SPRINT. The ¾-court sprint measures acceleration and running speed between two points. Beginning at the baseline of the basketball court, a player sprints to the farthest free throw line. Timing begins at the athlete's first movement and ends when any part of his or her body crosses the free throw line. If using a hand timer, take the average of three trials.

Explosive Measurements

A player's standing vertical jump is an excellent test of explosive power. It is the measurement of the height of a jump from both feet while extending the dominant arm.

STANDING VERTICAL JUMP. A player stands approximately 12 inches from the measuring apparatus with the dominant arm facing the measuring tool. With feet shoulder-width apart, he or she bends down slightly and draws extended arms behind the body. The athlete springs up, extending legs and arms simultaneously as he or she reaches up as far as possible with the dominant hand. The landing should be soft with knees bent. Note the highest point reached. Three trials may be allowed, with the highest of the three counting as the final result.

What Do You Search for in Players?

Every coach must have a clear understanding of the type of player that best fits into his or her system. In Activity 7.1, you will have the opportunity to create a list based on your philosophy. Two of the greatest coaches in the history of the game, Bob Knight and Pete Newell, listed their requirements in the following four statements:

1. I want a player who is willing to make a commitment to being as good as he can be each time that he plays.
2. I want a player who is willing and ready to do what has to be done to make a positive contribution in the most difficult of games.
3. I want a player who competes in each game as though there is nothing he will ever do that will be more important.
4. I want a player who, more than anything, wants our team to be the very best that it can be.

> *There is no substitute for talent. After that, I'm interested in his attitude. Is he coachable? Will he get along with the other players on the team? Is he selfish or unselfish? I want to know what his work habits are. I want to know about his character, his family background, and what kind of person he is.*
>
> —Lou Carnesecca, Naismith Basketball Hall of Fame Coach

Recruiting Is an Inexact Science

Coaches must accept the fact that recruiting is an inexact science. It is possible to do everything right in the recruiting process and still have the prospect select another school. It is also probable that you will sign a player who ultimately just doesn't fit in your program. As much as you try not to, you will make some recruiting mistakes, but for your longevity in the coaching profession, these mistakes must be kept at a minimum. Our advice is to have a systematic approach for recruiting and selecting players of high character who are a good match for both your basketball program and your university.

Selecting Assistant Coaches

Getting the right chemistry on your coaching staff is a must. Hire assistant coaches who share your same beliefs and values. They must be passionately devoted to the mission 24 hours a day, seven days a

"Marquette's coaching staff has done an outstanding job of preparing our players for the Big East Conference. Their energy, loyalty, and commitment have been key in our success."

—Tom Crean, Marquette University

week. This doesn't imply that an assistant coach has to work 24 hours a day, but it does mean that his or her passion doesn't get turned off and on.

Loyalty is an absolute necessity. Their job is to support and complement the head coach so the mission is accomplished. This doesn't mean being submissive or docile. Assistant coaches are expected to challenge the head coach if they think he or she is incorrect. Colin Powell explained loyalty to the people who reported to him in these words: "When we are debating an issue, loyalty means giving me an honest opinion, whether you think I'll like it or not. Disagreement, at this state, stimulates me. But once a decision is made, the debate ends. From that point on, loyalty means executing the decision as if it were your own."

Select assistant coaches with high energy. These individuals have the drive to get things done and are a source of enthusiasm every day. Outstanding assistants are excellent teachers and inspire others to work hard. They also have the personal courage to confront and correct players who are not adhering to the team's core values.

Assistant coaches cannot be oversensitive or let their egos get in the way of team success. They must demonstrate selfless service in every aspect of their job. Any jealousy among staff members is a cancer and must be cut out immediately.

Hire competent assistant coaches, match their strengths with the needs of the program, and then get out of their way. Let them do their job and then publicly recognize their good work. Prepare them for becoming head coaches by giving them a wide range of experiences such as scouting, scheduling, practice planning, game preparation, public speaking, academic counseling, and recruiting.

Mentoring assistant coaches and helping them reach their professional goals is an important responsibility of head coaches. One of the best head coaches in the nation for mentoring assistants is Tom Izzo. "I've always felt that part of my job is to give someone else the chance to get what I am getting," said Izzo.

During Izzo's first 10 years at Michigan State, six of his assistants became Division I head coaches. Izzo trusts his assistants. He gives them complete ownership of specific areas and then holds them accountable. They are expected to work hard and make an impact on the program. He develops a family environment with his staff and is like a one-man public relations firm when it comes to promoting assistants and helping them professionally.

Marquette has tried to model Michigan State's success in helping staff members become head coaches. Since 2000, four assistant coaches have become head coaches: Tod Kowalczyk at Wisconsin-Green Bay, Darrin Horn at Western Kentucky, Tim Buckley at Ball State, and Kyle Green at Lewis University.

Instant Replay

1. Successful teams are composed of talented team players.
2. Coaches should select players based on the team's core values.
3. Players lacking character will destroy team unity and team play.
4. Coaches should never overestimate their ability to change people of low character and selfishness into team players.
5. Loyalty is an absolute necessity when hiring assistant coaches.

Coach's Game Plan

ACTIVITY 7.1 Make a list of the qualities that you search for in a basketball player.

8

Promote Teamwork and Team Unity

Talent alone is not enough. They used to tell me you have to use your five best players, but I've found that you win with the five who fit together best.

—Red Auerbach, Naismith Basketball Hall of Fame Coach

Team success lies at the very heart of teamwork and team unity. Through teamwork, players coordinate their efforts, work together, and complement each other's play. Through team unity, players become focused on the same objectives and learn to trust one another. Great things happen when individuals are devoted to a cause greater than themselves. This chapter will present a smorgasbord of ideas that promote teamwork, unity, and team success.

> *The teams that win championships are the ones that play team basketball.*
>
> —Rick Barry, Naismith Basketball Hall of Fame Player

Team Ownership

Team ownership occurs when team members see themselves as an integral part of the basketball program. Five ways to promote team ownership are through shared values, game preparation, road rules, recruiting, and shared leadership.

Shared Values

An excellent way to develop team ownership is to include your players in the selection of the team's core values. Do this by having your team members select one of the core values each year. Players often have a clear understanding of what needs to be emphasized in order for the team to reach its potential. Allowing your players to contribute to the core values encourages commitment and unity.

Game Preparation

Players should be involved in the planning of their team's success. In 2004, Marquette players helped design the game plan for the opening Conference USA game against Houston. Players were split into groups of three and given different areas to watch as they studied game films of their opponent. Their job was to come up with strengths, weaknesses, and recommendations. It was an opportunity for players to learn the art of devising a game plan, but, more important, it forced players to work together off the floor for a common goal. They took ownership of the scouting report, the execution of the game plan, and the eventual win.

Road Rules

Winning on the road in college basketball is very difficult. An excellent way to unite a team on the road is to establish "road rules." Prior to the first Big East Conference road game against Seton Hall in 2006, the Marquette coaches and players created the following five "road rules":

1. Have fun/Team before me
2. Defensive transition/No easy baskets
3. Compete/Toughness wins
4. Own the boards
5. Execute under pressure/Make the extra pass

Each member of the team was instructed in the importance of his role. Assistant coach Jason Rabedeaux had lanyards made with the five road rules attached, and every coach and player wore his lanyard during the entire trip. It was a great way to promote team unity and reinforce the keys for winning on the road.

When a team is on the road, it is important to break up the cliques that often form on a team. One strategy is to randomly select the dinner companions for your team. To do this, divide your traveling party into squads. Each squad has three members. If there are 27 people in your traveling group, for example, there are nine squads. Twenty-seven tickets are put into a hat. Each ticket has a number on it ranging from one to nine. There are three tickets with number one, three tickets with number two, and so on. Every team member receives his meal money and then pulls a ticket out of the hat. The three players who have number one eat together. The players with number two eat together, and so forth. The members of each squad must pool their money together and decide where they want to eat. They don't have to order the same thing, but they must work together to make sure that it is fair and equal for all squad members. The coaching staff adds one additional requirement by designating a topic that each team member must discuss with his or her squad members. The discussion points can be anything that the coaches and team captains feel would be relevant and interesting. Examples of discussion points that have been used in the past are:

- My most influential high school teacher
- The NBA team that best characterizes team play and unselfishness
- What I like most about my hometown

Recruiting

Players should play an important role in the recruiting process. Their insight is very valuable in determining whether a recruit is the right fit for your program. When a recruit visits Marquette, he gets to know all the players on the team. We believe it is important that the recruit spends more time with the players than he does with the coaching staff. After all, he is going to play with the current players, and they're all going to live together.

Soon after the recruit leaves campus, the team members are asked if the prospect meets the criteria for a Marquette player. "There are times that we have had people visit campus that would not have fit in and we tell the coaching staff," said Steve Novak. "It is very important to bring in high-caliber people that are going to be good team players. I compare it to joining an unselfish family."

Shared Leadership

One of the goals of Marquette basketball is to help every person become a better leader so he can compete with the very best and succeed. Players are taught there are different stages of leadership. The first stage is followership. During this stage, players begin to realize all the things they don't know and then open themselves to the possibility of being remade into something more. Players discover they are becoming a part of something much bigger than they are. They learn to listen carefully and intensely. They begin to trust their teammates, and they learn how to compete.

Playing successfully on the floor is only part of the picture. Players begin seeing the game from a coach's perspective. They learn how to watch a game tape, read a scouting report, and recognize the most important statistics on a statistic sheet.

Players assume different leadership roles throughout their careers. The veterans help new players through the followership stage. They act as role models and mentors, enforcing the team's core values. They work with younger players to help improve their basketball skills. They learn leadership skills that will transfer into their careers after graduation.

To emphasize the importance of leadership, Marquette established the Dwyane Wade Legacy of Leadership Award in 2004. The award is presented annually to a player who most exemplifies the traits displayed by Wade during his years at Marquette.

The Dwyane Wade Legacy of Leadership Award is awarded annually to the Marquette player who demonstrates exemplary leadership qualities.

Define Roles

Defining roles is one of the most important jobs of a coach. It is crucial that every team member has a very clear and thorough understanding of his or her role and how that role fits into the overall mission of the program. This also includes understanding the responsibilities of teammates. It is impossible for players to work cooperatively with each other if they do not recognize each other's strengths.

All team members must work cooperatively with each other and understand each other's roles.

The key to teamwork is to learn a role, accept that role, and strive to become excellent playing it. Regardless of what role a player is asked to play, he or she must take that role and make it his or her masterpiece. As William Shakespeare once wrote, "Act well your part. Therein lies the glory."

Former Marquette and NBA star Glenn "Doc" Rivers made a great point when he spoke to Marquette's team in 2003, saying, "You don't get to move on to another role until you master the one that you are in."

NBA great Oscar Robertson believes that many NBA players lack the concept of role-playing. "Few players seem willing to be role players, to make a contribution off the bench, or actually earn more playing time," Robertson said. "They take their money and go home."

> *Most teams have guys that want to win, but aren't willing to do what it takes. What it takes is to give yourself over to the team and play your part. That may not always make you happy, but you've got to do it. Because when you do, that's when you win.*
>
> —Bill Cartwright, Former NBA Player and Coach

Getting players to have the desire to master the role they are in, but not become satisfied with it, is crucial. That is why summer leagues and individual workouts are so important. They give players an opportunity to improve their skills above and beyond their current role. Marquette's players separate themselves from the rest through individual instruction. This time is designed to help a player show constant improvement so that he can become the best team player possible.

Line of Commitment

Players must understand that practice begins the moment they walk onto the court. Some coaches actually paint a line that players must cross as they enter their practice site. Players are asked to think about and recommit to the team's core values before crossing the line. You may want to have a sign listing your core values on a wall adjacent to the line as a visual reminder for the players. Crossing the "line of commitment" signifies that a player is dedicated to the program's core values and is focused on the mission for that day.

Buddy System

The buddy system is an effective way to develop trust, unity, camaraderie, and unit cohesion. It can be a form of peer mentoring by matching the newcomers with veteran team members. The experienced players tutor their new teammates in the nuances of the game and the team's system. It sparks two-way communication and allows players to feed off each other's input and enthusiasm. Effective coaches capitalize on this enthusiasm and recognize that player-to-player learning is just as important as formal training.

Assigning roommates on road trips is another way to use the buddy system. Each person is responsible for making sure that his roommate is always at the right place at the right time during the course of the trip. To avoid cliques, it is important to change roommates throughout the season. If your coaching staff senses that two players are not getting along, assign them to be roommates and tell them to work it out. If they don't work it out, they are hurting the team's chances for success and that is unacceptable.

Some coaches don't like to confront controversy. Coaches must accept the fact there often will be conflicts among players because the game attracts people with strong ambition, strong personal pride, and large egos. At times it is difficult for these individuals to put aside their self-interest for the good of the team. Helping players reposition their egos is a never-ending job for coaches. When people come into your program with very high opinions of themselves, you must work with them to transfer their self-centeredness into a team-first mentality. Creating a buddy system helps players become accountable for not only their actions, but also those of their teammates.

Shrink the Circle

"Shrink the circle" is a phrase used to accentuate the importance of team togetherness. "Marquette's program is built on team togetherness," said Barb Kellaher, special assistant to the head coach. "The players live, eat, study, and play basketball together. But most important, they genuinely like and respect each other. They are initially forced into a regimented environment, but they quickly appreciate the extra discipline when trying to balance the demands of school and basketball. They form a bond with each other that will last a lifetime."

"Team togetherness begins in the summer when you first get to Marquette," explained Joe Chapman, four-year letter winner from 2003 through 2006. "As a team you do everything together whether

Successful teams create a family environment among all team members.

it is going out to dinner, going to the movies, working out, or just hanging out. It really starts off the court. We develop chemistry and a respect for each other that automatically transcends onto the court."

Team success depends on the people who are in your locker room every day. These are the individuals who are making the sacrifices and understand the team's mission. Marquette players are reminded every year to "shrink their circle." They are given little Frisbees to hang in their lockers to remind them of this important concept. The more recognition players receive, the more people will try and stretch their circles and get inside. It happens all the time in professional sports. If players aren't careful, their circles will eventually break, leaving them open and vulnerable.

Outside influences can be a distraction to a team. This can come from avid fans who desperately want to become friends with players in the limelight or from negative outsiders who quickly criticize the team when things go wrong. It is imperative that a team be a close-knit unit. Team members must know they can always depend on each other.

Peer Coaching

Another technique to improve team togetherness is through peer coaching. Divide your team into two squads and allow them to coach themselves during a five-minute period. You could do the same with late-game situations by designating a score and playing 30-second games. The main purpose is to provide opportunities for players to work together for a common goal and to stay united during difficult times.

Players at Marquette who are injured or sitting out for the year are expected to be student coaches. On game nights, they keep important statistics and they observe the action closely and keep the coaching staff informed. At times, these players will give their statistics to the team during a time-out. In fact, when Travis Diener was injured during his senior year, there were three or four time-outs when he did much of the talking. One of Dwyane Wade's responsibilities during his first year was to chart deflections, and he would share that information with the team during halftime. During the season that Dan Fitzgerald sat out, he kept track of how many times Marquette made three or more defensive stops in a row.

Stretch the Talent of Your Players

Effective coaches bring out the best in their team members. They understand that most people do not reach their goals because they are reluctant to take risks. Successful coaches lead players out of their comfort zones. They put players in situations where they have to deal with adversity and fight back.

> *The way to tap into that energy is not by being autocratic, but by working with the players and giving them increased responsibility to shape their roles.*
>
> —Phil Jackson, NBA Championship Coach

Dwyane Wade could not play or travel with the team during his first year at Marquette, but he was allowed to practice with the team and sit on the bench during home games. During that year, he learned how to push himself harder than he had in the past. In fact, there were several days when Wade was thrown out of practice because he was not maximizing his talent. He would coast at times, pick his moments to compete, and not always run the floor like he could. "At times I wanted to call home and say that I can't do this," said Wade. "But it made me stronger, and it made me really want it more."

Wade received excellent coaching from Jack Fitzgerald in high school, but he was somewhat of a natural scorer. At Marquette, he had to develop all the other fundamentals that would make him an all-around player, and he had to come back the next day and even do it better. This is the required standard for all players, especially the ones who have special talent. It is your job as a coach to make them better each day. The moment they back off and lose their hunger is the start of their decline. One of Wade's greatest legacies at Marquette is that he never got tired of getting better. He not only loves to play but more important, he really loves to work on his game and get better.

Do not shortchange your players and let them get by with less than a maximum effort. To help players improve, coaches must begin with the end in mind, even if the players don't see it. Frankly, it is not their job to see it. Their job is to see themselves get better step-by-step. It is the coach's responsibility to see the desired end.

Marquette brought in an exceptional recruiting class in the fall of 2005, and it was essential to establish a strong foundation so the newcomers could adjust to college life and Division I basketball quickly. The coaching staff introduced the program's core values and taught players how to hold each other accountable. The hardest thing when you have a younger team is to have them understand how important a defensive rebounding mentality is. You really try to teach players to hit singles, not home runs. The more they can make the simple play, the better it is. The players must also have a real distaste for losing. They have to gain the mentality that playing together and playing unselfishly help you win. It's exciting when you have players who really want to get better.

"When you get here [Marquette]," said Jerel McNeal, "people push you to the max. They bring everything out of you that's possible to get. I have been blessed with a lot of physical gifts, but I think everything else is just heart and understanding how to play defense."

McNeal injected a sense of fearlessness and aggressiveness into the Marquette line-up. He grabbed 12 rebounds against the University of Connecticut, and his versatility and aggressiveness allow him to drive to the basket and finish plays.

Big East 2006 Rookie of the Year Dominic James said, "Our talent took us a long way in high school. But there's so much more you've got to learn on the college level. There are things you can get away with in high school that you're not going to be able to get away with in college. The most important aspect of college basketball has been being a student of the game more than anything else. You can no longer go out there and just beat people on your talent. You have to know the game."

"You've got to work hard to keep your grades up," added Wesley Matthews, who was named Mr. Basketball for Wisconsin in 2005. "But outside of that, it's understanding the college concepts. Just the little things that you never did in high school but have to do now. Like the different kinds of stances you have on defense. How you go across a screen. We have to read three different types of screens and how we're going to run and chase our man off each one."

From a team perspective, there are many ways that a coach can extend a team. One of the best ways is to put players in situations where they have to depend on their teammates, such as having five offensive players go against seven defenders. This strategy was used in Marquette's practices prior to their upset of No. 2 Connecticut in the Big East Conference opener in 2006.

Another way to do this is to place a limit on the number of dribbles that can be used. Restrict your players to only one dribble and have them play a full-court scrimmage. They learn very quickly that they must work hard to create open passing lanes for their teammates. It takes excellent teamwork to advance the ball and get an open shot.

Off the court, a good place to stretch the talents of players and make team members depend on each other is in the weight room. "Probably the most important things that our strength and conditioning staff brings to the basketball program go beyond the physi-

"Teams form as players go through hard times together. Our strength and conditioning staff puts players in difficult situations where they have to rely on each other."

—Scott Holsopple, Head Strength and Conditioning Coach, Marquette University

cal conditioning of our players," explained Scott Holsopple, Marquette's head strength and conditioning coach. "We establish partners with one player on the leg press and the other on the stationary bike. The player on the leg press cannot stop until his partner goes two miles on the bike. If the person on the leg press quits before his partner reaches two miles, the biker must ride an additional one-half mile. They quickly learn the importance of working hard and not letting their teammate down. Trust also forms because each player knows that his teammate is working as hard as he can."

Thought for the Day

Many successful coaches use daily themes during the season to reinforce their core values. At North Carolina, Coach Dean Smith's players received a daily practice plan with a "Thought for the Day" and the "Emphasis of the Day" at the top of the page. The "Thought for the Day" was usually a philosophical statement that put basketball into a larger context. Smith used the Serenity Prayer on occasion or a statement such as "Don't let one day pass without doing something for a person who cannot repay you." The "Emphasis of the Day" was a basketball thought such as "sprint back on defense."

Smith started each practice with a few comments and then selected a player to either recite the "Thought for the Day" or the "Emphasis for the Day." Players knew that it was their responsibility to learn these prior to practice. If for any reason a player failed to give the correct response, the entire team had to run. Players made sure they learned the "Thought for the Day" and the "Emphasis for the Day" because they didn't want their teammates to run for their mistake.

Team Communication

There must be two-way communication among all team members for a program to be successful. You can't rely on one or two players; every player must talk on both ends of the court. There is no close second to team members talking with one another. It is an ongoing process and one of the most frustrating and challenging parts of building a team. You must work on communication every day.

The players on the 2003 Marquette Final Four Team were outstanding communicators. Travis Diener, Dwyane Wade, and Robert Jackson led the way with the talking on the floor. That enabled Todd Townsend, Scott Merritt, Terry Sanders, and Steve Novak to gain confidence.

The premier program in the country for team communication is Duke University. The coaching staff at Marquette considers Mike Krzyzewski's program the gold standard and is always searching for ways to get our program to that level. The night before Marquette's game against Seton Hall in 2006, the players watched videotape showing Duke's players communicating to each other on the court. It was a five-minute collection of clips showing what team communication looks like when it is done correctly.

Five ways to improve team communication are by making eye contact, pointing to the passer, standing for a teammate, forming team huddles, and soliciting input from players.

Make Eye Contact

Eye-to-eye contact between the speaker and the listener is a requirement for all Marquette team members. This is expected on the basketball court and in the classroom.

Players are expected to give their undivided attention to the person speaking.

When Joe Chapman joined the Golden Eagles in 2002, he listened, but kept his head turned away or looked at the floor. The coaches worked with him and helped him understand that good communication begins with eye contact. It is a sign of respect and conveys an openness to listen to others.

"I came from the South Side of Chicago and I didn't have a father figure," said Chapman. "The coaching staff embraced me as one of their own and taught me so many things, such as how to look someone in their eyes when you talk with them. They insisted on players showing respect to authority figures and veteran players."

Point to the Passer

Many coaches make it a rule that the player who scores must acknowledge the passer by pointing in his or her direction. This practice was conceived in the mid-1960s when Hall of Fame coaches John Wooden and Dean Smith attended a Fellowship of Christian Athletes conference in Colorado. Wooden mentioned to Smith that he wanted the receiver of a pass to say "thank you" to the passer, or give a quick wink. Smith agreed with the concept but wanted a more visible gesture so fans could appreciate the passer. He asked his players to acknowledge the pass by pointing at the passer.

During the 1972 season, North Carolina All-American Bobby Jones started a new point-to-the-passer ritual when, during a game, he received a pass from a teammate but missed a fast-break layup. Jones still turned to the passer and acknowledged the good pass. Dean Smith added this to his list of expectations and called it the "Bobby Jones rule."

First Team All-Big East Conference performer Steve Novak hit a school-record 121 three-pointers in 2006. Steve was a humble star who always acknowledged the passer. "One thing about Steve," said point guard Dominic James, "is that every time you pass him the ball, after he hits the shot he will always point or say 'nice pass.' It is the little things such as this that make a difference in team unity."

Stand for a Teammate

When a player is taken out of a game, every player seated on the bench shows his or her appreciation by standing and applauding. This gesture demonstrates respect and unselfishness and is not optional. It makes no difference how long someone was in the game or how well someone played.

Teammates also are expected to rush over and help a player up from the floor after he takes a charge or dives on the court in pursuit of a loose ball. It is another way to recognize hustle plays and show appreciation for a player's tenacity.

Form Team Huddles

During time-outs or short breaks in the game, Marquette players are expected to quickly form a team huddle. We want to keep our huddles private, so we use the phrase "close it up," which means that players join together with their arms around each other. During a team huddle, all eyes are on the person speaking.

A key point in Duke's communication system is that players understand that these huddles serve an important purpose. It is a time to identify mistakes and reinforce team strategy. Coach Krzyzewski demands that "only the truth can be spoken" during these huddles. When things aren't going as planned, corrections must be

Whenever a player ends up on the court,
teammates are expected to help him to his feet.

During all time-outs, Marquette players join together with arms around each other.

made immediately. When things are running smooth, it is time to compliment and encourage others to keep up the good work.

Solicit Input

Soliciting input from team members strengthens a team by allowing players to take ownership. Don't be afraid to ask your players tough questions such as to identify what is keeping the team from reaching its potential. Players often have a clear understanding of what needs to be emphasized in order for the team to be successful. An example of a team survey can be found at the end of this chapter in the Coach's Game Plan. Surveys such as this one provide players with the opportunity to identify team strengths as well as weaknesses. This information is critical because it presents the player's perception and identifies areas that must be addressed.

Outside Speakers

An excellent way to promote teamwork and team unity is to bring in guests to speak with your team. Through their wealth of experiences, these individuals can capture the attention of your players and reinforce your core values. Outside coaches, administrators, professors, professional athletes, priests, former players, community leaders, business executives, and military leaders have spoken to the players at Marquette.

On several occasions Lt. Gen. Hal Moore, Battalion Commander of the 7th Cavalry during the first major battle in the Vietnam War, spoke about the importance of taking care of teammates. He discussed the importance of this speech, which he gave his soldiers the day before leading them to war:

We are moving into the Valley of the Shadow of Death where you will watch the back of the man next to you, as he will watch yours, and you won't care what color he is, or by what name he calls God. We are going into battle against a tough and determined enemy. I can't promise you that I will bring you all home alive. But this I swear . . . when we go into battle, I will be the first to step on the field and I will be the last to step off. And I will leave no one behind . . . dead or alive. We will all come home together.

In the coaches' workroom at Marquette is an autographed poster from General Moore. It serves as a constant reminder to lead by example, demand the best, and take care of all team members.

Spotlighting

Spotlighting is a technique that can be used to recognize players and promote team unity. Have a coach or a player make a positive statement about another teammate in front of the entire team. Time can be set aside to spotlight teammates before, during, or after practice.

An example of post-practice spotlighting would be to have a coach identify a player for something the athlete did during practice that modeled one of the core values of the program. In turn, that player would be asked to spotlight another teammate. Spotlighting works best by identifying certain themes for the day or the week. Tell the team the theme ahead of time and then have players look for teammates exhibiting these qualities.

Instant Replay

1. Team success lies at the very heart of teamwork and team unity.
2. Five ways to promote team ownership are shared values, game preparation, road rules, recruiting, and shared leadership.
3. The key to teamwork is to learn a role, accept that role, and strive to become excellent playing it.
4. Successful coaches put players in situations where they have to deal with adversity and fight back.
5. Every player must talk on both ends of the court.
6. Five ways to improve team communication are: make eye contact, point to the passer, stand for a teammate, form team huddles, and solicit input.
7. Soliciting input from team members strengthens a team because it allows players to take ownership.

Coach's Game Plan

ACTIVITY 8.1 Do a team survey. One way to solicit input from your players is to have them answer these questions:

1. What do you like most about this team?
2. What one thing is keeping this team from being even better?
3. What four or five words would you use to describe this team?
4. What is your biggest source of frustration with the team right now?

3

Why Teams Win

Being a winner in basketball comes down to three things: conditioning, fundamentals, and teamwork.

—Bill Sharman, Naismith Basketball Hall of Fame Player and Coach

Championships are won when players sacrifice personal glory for the welfare of the team.

9

Statistical Factors That Determine Winning and Losing

If it moves—chart it.

—Jack Gardner, Naismith Basketball Hall of Fame Coach

Basketball coaches are continually searching for information that could give them an advantage over an opponent. Hall of Fame coach Jack Gardner believed "details win games" and was one of the first coaches to use statisticians to compile precise charts on every phase of the game. Gardner's office at the University of Utah was referred to as a Basketball Library of Congress during the 1960s because there were neatly bound files containing game-by-game, minute-by-minute analysis of everything that had happened during Gardner's coaching career.

In 1978, authorities from the National Association of Basketball Coaches and various Division I conferences recognized the need to analyze basketball statistics in order to determine which factors were the most important in winning and losing games. If certain factors could be shown to contribute to team success, the offensive and defensive philosophies of coaches could be based on scientific evidence rather than on past experiences or mass opinions.

1978 Research Study

Co-author Pim investigated 316 games played in five Division I conferences during the 1978 season. Fifteen statistical factors were selected for study, and the data were collected for every conference game played in the five conferences: Atlantic Coast, Big 8, Big 10, Southwest Athletic, and Western Athletic.

The results of the study revealed two combinations of variables that significantly differentiate between winning and losing teams. The variables of field goal percentage, free throws attempted, total rebounds, personal fouls, and halftime lead best discriminated winning teams from losing teams when all 316 games were statistically tested. The variables of field goal percentage, total rebounds, and personal fouls best differentiated winning and losing teams when the five conferences were statistically treated singularly.

Based on the findings of the study, coaches should utilize practice sessions specifically designed to improve field goal percentage, rebounding techniques, and the ability to draw fouls.

2005 Research Study

In 2005, co-author Pim along with Maj. Artie Coughlin, Dr. Lynn Fielitz, and Ed Fry, boy's basketball coach at Crescent High School in

Iva, South Carolina, conducted a sequel to the 1978 study, analyzing 477 conference games in these five conferences: Atlantic Coast, Southeastern, Big 12, Big 10, and Conference USA.

In this study, 20 statistical variables were investigated to determine which factors were the most important in determining winning and losing teams in college basketball. The statistical factors studied were:

- Points scored
- Field goals made
- Field goals attempted
- Field goal percentage
- Three-point field goals made
- Three-point field goals attempted
- Three-point field goal percentage
- Free throws made
- Free throws attempted
- Free throw percentage
- Offensive rebounds
- Defensive rebounds
- Total rebounds
- Personal fouls
- Assists
- Turnovers
- Blocked shots
- Steals
- Halftime lead
- Location of game

Results

The following findings are based on the data from 477 conference games.

- **Field goals made.** Winning teams averaged 3.3 more field goals made per game than losing teams. In winning performances the mean number of field goals made was 25.71 while in losing performances the mean number of field goals made was 22.41.

- **Field goals attempted.** Losing teams averaged 0.73 more field goal attempts per game than the winning teams. In winning performances, the mean number of field goal attempts per game was 54.54 while in losing performances the mean number of field goal attempts was 55.27.
- **Field goal percentage.** The five conference totals indicated that the field goal shooting percentages of winning teams were 6.7 percentage points higher than the field goal shooting percentages of losing teams. The mean field goal percentage in winning performances was 47.4 while in losing performances the mean field goal percentage was 40.7. The team that recorded the higher field goal shooting percentage was the winner in 356 of 477 games, or 74.6 percent.
- **Three-point field goals made.** In winning performances the mean number of three-point field goals made was 7.10 while in losing performances the mean number of three-point field goals made was 5.98.
- **Three-point field goals attempted.** Losing teams averaged 0.75 more three-point field goal attempts per game than the winning teams. In winning performances, the mean number of three-point field goal attempts per game was 18.27 while in losing performances the mean number of three-point field goal attempts was 19.02.
- **Three-point field goal percentage.** The five conference totals indicated that the three-point field goal shooting percentages of winning teams were 7.66 percentage points higher than the three-point field goal shooting percentages of losing teams. The mean three-point field goal percentage in winning performances was 38.61 while in losing performances the mean three-point field goal percentage was 30.95.
- **Free throws made.** Winning teams averaged 4.3 more free throws made per game than losing teams. In winning performances the mean number of free throws made per game was 16.32 while in losing performances the mean number of free throws made was 12.06. In 333 of 477 games, or 69.81 percent, the team that scored the most free throws was the eventual winner.

- **Free throws attempted.** Winning teams averaged 5.1 more free throw attempts per game than losing teams. The mean number of free throws attempted per game by winning teams was 23.01 while losing teams attempted an average of 17.91 free throws per game.
- **Free throw percentage.** In winning performances the mean free throw percentage was 70.65 while in losing performances the mean free throw percentage was 67.21.
- **Offensive rebounds.** In winning performances the mean number of offensive rebounds per game was 11.52 while in losing performances the mean number of offensive rebounds per game was 11.35.
- **Defensive rebounds.** The winning teams averaged 3.68 more defensive rebounds per game than the losing teams. In winning performances the mean number of defensive rebounds per game was 24.41 while in losing performances the mean number of defensive rebounds per game was 20.73.
- **Total rebounds.** The winning teams averaged 3.85 more rebounds per game than the losing teams. In winning performances the mean number of rebounds per game was 35.94 while in losing performances the mean number of rebounds per game was 32.08. The team that grabbed the higher number of rebounds was the winner in 310 of 477 contests, or 64.99 percent.
- **Personal fouls.** The winning teams averaged 2.59 fewer personal fouls per game than the losing teams. In winning performances the mean number of personal fouls per game was 17.46 as compared to 20.05 in losing performances. The team that committed the higher number of personal fouls was the eventual winner in only 120 of the 477 contests, or 25.16 percent.
- **Assists.** The winning teams averaged 3.36 more assists per game than the losing teams. The mean number of assists per game in winning performances was 15.14 while in losing performances the mean number of assists per game was 11.78.
- **Turnovers.** In winning performances the mean number of turnovers per game was 12.98 while in losing performances the mean number of turnovers per game was 14.69. The winning teams averaged 1.71 fewer turnovers per game than the losing teams.

- **Blocked shots.** The mean number of blocked shots per game in winning performances was 3.73 while in losing performances the mean was 2.97.
- **Steals.** The mean number of steals per game in winning performances was 7.57 while in losing performances the mean was 6.09. The winning teams averaged 1.48 more steals per game than the losing teams.
- **Halftime lead.** The team that held the point advantage at halftime was the eventual winner in 352 of 477 games, or 73.79 percent.
- **Location of game.** The home team was the eventual winner in 307 of the 477 contests, or 64.36 percent. The percentage of home court wins in the five conferences was 63.22 in the Atlantic Coast, 68.75 in the Southeastern, 63.54 in the Big 12, 67.05 in the Big 10, and 60.00 in Conference USA.

Conclusions

The 2005 study revealed five statistical variables that best predict team success in college basketball. Field goal percentage, free throws made, total rebounds, personal fouls, and halftime lead best discriminated winning teams from losing teams when all 477 games were statistically tested. (See Table 9.1.)

TABLE 9.1 Most Important Factors in Winning College Basketball Games

---

1. Field goal percentage

2. Free throws made

3. Personal fouls

4. Total rebounds

5. Halftime lead

Source: Pim, Coughlin, Fielitz, Fry (2005)

Implementation

Based on the findings of the study, coaches should utilize practice sessions specifically designed to improve field goal percentage, rebounding techniques, and the ability to draw fouls. Defensively, coaches should devise strategies to limit their opponents' high-percentage shot opportunities. This includes transition baskets, second-shot opportunities, and free throws.

Chapters 10 and 11 will help coaches design practices that reinforce the most important factors in determining team success.

Instant Replay

1. The variables of field goal percentage, free throws made, total rebounds, personal fouls, and halftime lead best discriminated winning teams from losing teams in 477 conference games played during the 2005 season in the Atlantic Coast, Southeastern, Big 12, Big 10, and Conference USA.
2. The team that recorded the higher field goal percentage was the winner in 75 percent of the games.
3. The team that scored the most free throws was the eventual winner in 70 percent of the games.
4. The team that recovered the higher number of rebounds was the winner 65 percent of the time.
5. The team that committed the higher number of personal fouls was the eventual winner in only 25 percent of the games.
6. The team that held the point advantage at halftime was the winner 74 percent of the time.

10

Offensive Keys for Team Success

All I ever did at Marquette University was to make five people one.

—Al McGuire, Naismith Basketball Hall of Fame Coach

Successful coaches identify factors that best determine team success and design their practices so their players become proficient in these areas. Offensively, the two most important factors are getting high-percentage shots and making your opponent commit personal fouls.

The goal at Marquette is to shoot least at 25
free throws every game.

To succeed in both of these areas, players must learn how to attack
the basket in transition and the half-court game. This chapter dis-
cusses techniques that maximize a team's ability to get more free
throw attempts and shoot high-percentage shots.

Get to the Free Throw Line

Personal fouls play a major role in determining the winning and losing teams in basketball. Winning teams generally shoot more free
throws. They get to the free throw line because they are committed
to inside play, dribble penetration, offensive rebounding, and transition basketball. Every personal foul, potentially, makes your opponent less aggressive and creates free throw shooting opportunities for
your team.

There are two important goals at Marquette regarding free throws.
The first goal is to shoot 25 or more free throws every game. The second goal is to be in the bonus situation by the 12-minute mark of

Team success depends on establishing an inside game.

each half. During the past four years, Marquette has not lost a game when they accomplished the latter goal. In 2003, Marquette's Final Four team accomplished this feat nine times.

In the 2006 NBA Finals, the victorious Miami Heat averaged 34.5 free throw attempts while Dallas only went to the free throw line 25.8 times per game. A deciding factor was Dwyane Wade's ability to dribble penetrate and get fouled. Wade averaged 16 free throw attempts per game.

Pass the Ball Inside

Team success depends on scoring from inside the lane. These are often called paint points because the area inside the free throw lane is referred to as the paint. One way to generate paint points is to pass the ball inside to post players.

When posting up, establish a stance as close to
the basket as possible with the defender out of
the passing lane.

*It doesn't matter who scores the points. It's who gets the ball
to the scorer.*

—Larry Bird, Naismith Basketball Hall of Fame Player

Floor Location

Great post players receive the ball in a high-scoring area with at least
one foot in the lane. Pat Summitt and her coaching staff at Tennessee
use the terms "double bury" and "single bury" to describe the desired
floor locations for a post player.

- "Double bury" is when a post player has both feet deeply
  imbedded in the paint and the post defender is sealed from the
  passing lane.
- "Single bury" is when a post player has one foot in the paint
  and the post defender is sealed from the passing lane.

- A perimeter player must pass inside to a post player who has established either a "double bury" position or a "single bury" position.

Post-Up Stance

To become strong inside scorers, it is essential players learn how to establish an inside position that keeps post defenders out of the passing lane. When posting up, a player must initiate contact with the post defender with his or her legs, buttocks, back, shoulders, and upper arms to keep the defensive player in place. A teaching cue to emphasize is "sit on the defender's legs." Key elements in the post-up stance are:

- Maintain a wide base with a low center of gravity.
- Square the shoulders to the passer. The passer must see both the numbers and the letters on the front of the post player's

The post player should maintain a wide base with the elbows out and parallel to the floor. The passer should see the front numbers and the letters on the post player's jersey.

jersey. There should be no part of the defender's body that interferes with the passer's vision of these two things.

- Keep both arms up and elbows parallel to the floor. There is a slight bend in the elbow, and the post player should be able to see the back of his or her hands.
- Present a two-hand target with fingers spread and pointing upward.
- Do not allow the defensive player to get his or her foot or arm in the passing lane.

Read the Post Defender and the Ball Handler

It is important for post players to read their defenders to determine how they are being guarded. They must also focus their attention on the position of the ball handler. When on the same side of the court as the ball handler, the post player should be on an imaginary line through the ball and the basket, as shown in the following illustration. This is called getting "on track" with the passer. It shortens the pass from the post feeder and provides the best passing angle.

The best way to read a post defender is through "sight and radar." Sight involves using the eyes to locate not only the defender but also openings in the defense. Radar involves using the legs, hips, buttocks, and arms to feel the location of the post defender. There are four main ways an offensive post player can be defended—from behind, in front, side-front from the high side, or side-front from the low side. The following guidelines will help a post player score more effectively:

- If defended from behind, the post player should establish contact, keep the defender in place, and post up.
- If fronted, the post player should move closer to the ball and look for the lob pass or ball reversal.
- If defended on the high side, the post player should take the defender a step or two higher and post up.

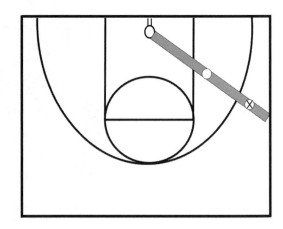

- If defended on the low side, the post player should take the defender a step or two lower and post up.

Seal the Post Defender

Post players must be able to maintain an open passing lane for at least two or three seconds so the passer can get them the ball. The two types of seals are the "leg whip" and the "pin and spin."

- The "leg whip" is simply taking one leg and whipping it in front of the defender in order to create an open passing lane.
- Stepping in between the defender's feet and executing a reverse pivot so that the defensive player is on the backside is called the "pin and spin."
- Post players must have active feet. They keep their feet alive with short, choppy steps and do not allow the defender to get a foot in front.

Catch the Pass and Read the Defense

The number one mistake post players make is moving too quickly after receiving the pass. A point of emphasis for post players should be "lower and slower." Here are important teaching points for catching the ball in the post and reading the defense:

- The pass inside to the post player should be caught with two hands and immediately brought to a position under the chin with the elbows out for protection. The teaching cue to emphasize is "chin it."
- As the ball is caught, the post player should lower his or her center of gravity four to six inches, look over the shoulder, and locate the defender.
- If the post player sees more than one-half of the post defender's body, he or she should go the opposite direction.

Take the Ball to the Basket Strong

Post players must execute strong, quick moves to the basket and expect physical contact. They should use head and shot fakes, if necessary, and always look for open teammates if they are double-teamed. Key points for taking the ball to the basket are:

The post player should catch the ball with two hands and immediately "chin it."

- Use the body to protect the ball.
- Concentrate on the basket.
- Use one quick, low dribble when using a dribble.
- Be quick without hurrying.
- Take the ball up with two hands.
- Shoot with the hand farthest from the defender.
- Use the backboard whenever possible.

Feeding the Post Player

A perimeter passer must read the defense and always pass away from the post defender. The passer must see both the defender and the hands of the receiver. Key teaching points for feeding the post player are:

- Use fakes to create open passing lanes. The teaching cue to emphasize is "to make a pass, you have to fake a pass."
- Use the dribble to establish a better passing angle.
- Deliver the pass only when the post player is open. The ball

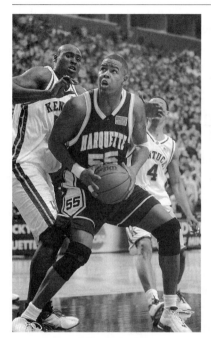

Locate the post defender, use the body to protect the ball, and shoot with the hand farthest from the defensive player.

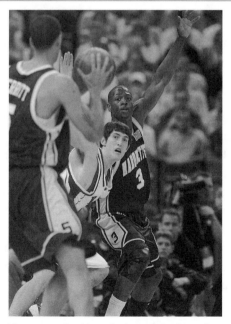

The passer should see both the defender and the hands of the potential receiver.

handler must see the post player's hands and the numbers and letters on the front of his or her jersey.

- Do not wind up when passing to a post player.

Offensive Rebounding

The importance of offensive rebounding cannot be overemphasized. Attacking the offensive boards produces high-percentage shots, more free throws, and a distinct psychological advantage over the defense. Teams increase their chances of winning by getting more than one shot each possession. The general rule of offensive rebounding is that a team will score on 50 percent of their second-shot attempts and 80 percent of their third-shot attempts. We believe in sending four players to the offensive glass at all times. Three players create a rebounding triangle, and the fourth player moves to a rebounding position on the weak side. The point guard is the designated player back, but we have rotation rules in case this player drives or is in the corner. Here are key points when teaching offensive rebounding:

- Remember that offensive rebounding is a state of mind. Outstanding rebounders possess the qualities of anticipation, determination, and hustle.
- Emphasize that rebounding is 75 percent desire and 25 percent ability.
- Assume that every shot will be missed and always keep hands up in a ready position.
- Hustle for the rebound. A "sprint to the glass mentality" is the number one key to successful offensive rebounding.
- Establish inside position by making the second and third effort. Do not run into the backs of the players who are attempting to block out.
- Establish weak side rebounding position. A missed shot from the wing or corner will be rebounded on the weak side approximately 70 percent of the time.
- Play heads up. The timing of a rebounder's jump is more important than the height.

Offensive rebounding demoralizes your opponent and is the best way for your team to get more shots.

—Bailey Howell, Naismith Basketball Hall of Fame Player

See the Floor and Read the Defense

Good players learn how to use their peripheral vision to see the court and find open teammates for high-percentage shots. Hall of Fame coach Bob Knight differentiates between the words *look* and *see*. "When you face the basket with the ball, you have to 'see,'" said Knight. "Anyone can 'look.' But it takes a player to 'see' what is going

The triple-threat position is the cornerstone for offensive basketball fundamentals.

on. Seeing the game involves three things: recognition, anticipation, and execution."

Great players always play with their heads up. They see their teammates and recognize their floor position and readiness for a pass. They also see the floor position of the defensive player guarding the potential receiver.

After receiving a pass on the perimeter, players should "catch and face" their basket and put the ball in the "triple-threat position." This position is the cornerstone of all offensive basketball fundamentals and enables players to quickly shoot, pass, or dribble the ball. The teaching cue for helping players see the floor in the correct sequence is "rim, post, and action."

- **See the rim.** First, look for a shot possibility or a pass to an open teammate under the basket.
- **See the post area.** Second, see if there is a pass to a post player available, a driving line to the basket, or a teammate cutting into the lane area.
- **See the entire action.** Third, see the entire floor. Look for scoring options such as a cutter using an off-the-ball screen, a shooter coming off a staggered screen, or a teammate clearing out.

Dribble Penetration

The premier guards in the game today create scoring opportunities for themselves or their teammates through dribble penetration. Whenever the ball gets inside the defense, the result is normally either a high-percentage shot or a foul on one of the defenders.

Players that are excellent drivers always see the floor and never dribble into trouble. They use fakes to get the ball defender out of the driving line. (The driving line is an imaginary straight line from the ball handler to the basket.) Two keys in dribble penetration are getting past the first line of defense and then locating and beating the second-line defenders. Successful dribble penetration depends on the ability of the driver to read the defense. Broadcaster Dick Vitale calls great penetrating guards "3-D players" because they are able to drive into the lane, draw more than one defender, and dish to the open player.

- When the driving line is free of defenders, the ball handler should drive to the basket and score. This is called "penetrate and score."
- When the defender of a teammate positioned on the perimeter picks up the dribbler, the ball handler should penetrate and pass to the open player on the perimeter. This is called "penetrate and kick."
- When a post defender steps up to stop the dribbler, the ball handler should pass inside to an open teammate. This is called "penetrate and dish."
- When attacking zone defenses, the ball handler should attack the gap between two defenders with a quick penetration dribble. Getting two defensive players moving toward the ball handler creates an open teammate.

Setting Screens

Screening is positioning a player in the path of a defender in order to create open looks at the basket and/or defensive mismatches. When setting a screen, the teaching cue is "loud, low, and legal." "Loud" signifies the sound of the feet hitting the court. Screeners should come to a jump stop with their feet shoulder-width apart approximately an arm's-length away from the defender. "Low" means the screener lowers his or her center of gravity by bending the knees, and "legal" reminds the screener to be firmly set and not moving. The following points are important when setting a screen off the ball:

- Assume a wide stance.
- Establish the proper screening angle. The screener's back should be square to the area where the cutter will receive the pass.
- Hold the screen.
- React to the defender and the cutter. When the defender attempts to fight through the screen, the player using the screen

will usually be open. When the defenders switch, the screener will be open.

• After setting the screen, turn toward the ball with the hands up.

Perhaps the most important part of offensive basketball is the part played by each man without the ball.

—John Wooden, Naismith Basketball Hall of Fame Coach

Receiving Screens

One of the biggest mistakes players make when receiving screens is cutting too soon. Pat Summitt wants the players setting the screens to call out their teammate's name and yell "wait, wait, wait," because she believes it is better to be a second late than to break too early. The player receiving the screen should go hip-to-hip and shoulder-to-shoulder off the screener and have his or her hands up anticipating a pass. The following are key teaching points when using an off-the-ball screen:

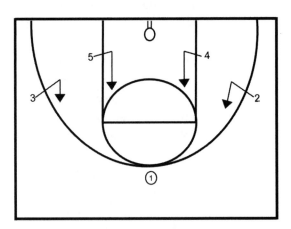

• Set up the defender with a "V" cut prior to using the screen.

• Wait for the screen. Give the screener time to get set. The teaching cue is "fake slow, break fast."

• Cut directly off the screen. The teaching cue is "hip-to-hip and shoulder-to-shoulder."

• Read the defense.

• Be ready for the pass and anticipate a scoring opportunity. The teaching cue is "hunt the shot."

Screens-on-the-Ball

When executed properly, the screen-on-the-ball is extremely difficult to defend and often creates mismatches in height or speed against teams that switch. The success of the screen-on-the-ball depends on the ability of the screener and the ball handler to read the defense.

- When the defender attempts to fight over the screen: when X1 attempts to stay with 1 and fight over the screen, 1 looks to turn the corner and drive to the basket for either a layup or an open jump shot.

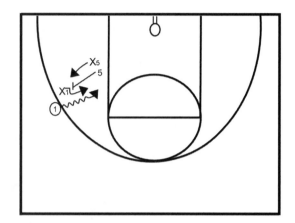

- When the defender goes below the screen: when X1 goes below 5's screen and X5 creates space for 1 to use the screen and look for the shot.

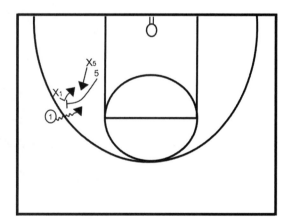

- When the defenders switch: when defensive players X1 and X5 switch on the screen, 1 takes two dribbles past the screen and looks to pass to 5 rolling to the basket. 5 rolls to the basket by pivoting on the inside foot and puts a target hand in the air. 5 should never lose sight of the ball. Note that 5 has inside position against the smaller defensive guard X1. This action is called the "pick-and-roll" and is used to combat the defensive switch.

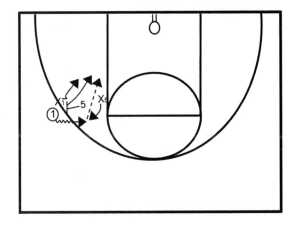

The pick-and-roll is the most difficult play to stop.

- When the screener's defender drops back: when X5 drops back to allow X1 to slide through 5's screen, 5 "pops" to the wing and looks for an open shot. This action is called the "pick and pop."

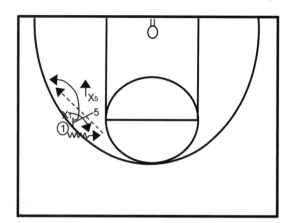

- When the screener's defender steps out early: when X5 steps out early in an attempt to slow down 1, 5 releases early and makes a direct cut to the basket. 1 passes to 5 cutting to the basket. This action is called the "slip."

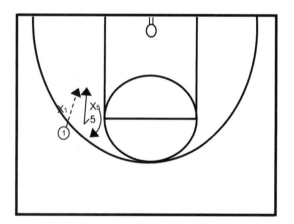

- When the defenders trap the ball handler: when both defenders X1 and X5 trap the ball handler, 1 uses a pull-back or retreat dribble to create space and pass to 5. This creates an offensive advantage because the defense will be outnumbered.

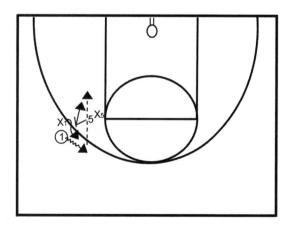

Shooters must be balanced and take shots within their range.

Take Good Shots

Successful teams generally attempt more shots and shoot a higher field goal percentage than their opponents. For this to happen, each player must understand proper shot selection. Knowing when not to shoot is just as important as knowing when to shoot. One of the more difficult tasks of a coach is teaching shot discipline. Coaches must assist players in learning their shooting ranges by keeping accurate statistics and charting shooting drills. Players should adhere to the following guidelines for shot selection:

- Be within your shooting range.
- Be well balanced and have a good look at the basket.
- Make sure no teammate has a better shot.
- Check that the rebounding areas are covered.
- Be sure the score and time indicate a need for this shot.

Protect the Ball

Winning teams generally commit fewer turnovers than their opponent. One of the tenets of Hall of Fame coach John Chaney's basketball philosophy is to protect the ball at all times. He detests turnovers and wants his team to average fewer than 10 turnovers per game. Chaney preaches that ball possession creates scoring opportunities, while turnovers are nothing more than wasted opportunities. Guidelines for reducing turnovers include:

- Always catch the ball with two hands.
- Meet all passes and watch the ball into your hands.
- When receiving a pass on the perimeter, quickly establish the triple-threat position.
- Never expose the ball to a defender.
- When receiving a pass in the post, chin the ball immediately.
- Before passing, see both the defender and the hands of your potential receiver.
- Always throw the ball to the side away from the defender.
- Use fakes to create open passing lanes.
- Throw accurate and timely passes.
- Always dribble with a purpose.
- Dribble with the hand farthest from the defender.
- Never pick up your dribble without a pass or a shot.
- Do not dribble into trouble.

Create Outnumbering Situations

One of the best ways to generate scoring opportunities is by creating situations in which the offensive players outnumber the defenders. This is best accomplished by fast-break basketball. Teams that fast break continually put pressure on their opponent's defense, and they look to fast break as soon as they gain possession of the basketball. The following are important teaching points for the fast break:

- The outlet pass is the key to initiating the fast break. The two-handed overhead pass is best to clear the ball out quickly after securing a rebound. After a made shot, the inbounds passer must sprint to the ball, see the floor, move quickly away from underneath the backboard, and make a crisp pass to an open teammate.
- The outlet players must read the defense and receive the pass as deep as possible. After receiving the pass, the outlet player should either pass ahead to an open teammate or advance the ball using a speed dribble. Get the ball into the middle of the floor whenever possible.
- The players filling the outside lanes must stay wide and look over their shoulders, anticipating a pass. They should spot up at the wings, approximately at the NBA three-point line.
- The fourth player down the floor sprints to the ball side block and calls for the ball.
- The last player down the floor either spots up on the perimeter or crashes the offensive boards on a shot attempt.

Maintain Proper Floor Balance

One of the most important concepts in offensive basketball is proper floor balance. The following illustration shows the ideal spacing between players is 15 to 18 feet. It is impossible to maintain proper spacing at all times because of the many screens being set, but it is important to always balance the floor after screening or cutting. Coaches must continually emphasize proper spacing and the correct distance perimeter players should be from the basket. An excellent way to do this is to use the NBA three-point line in practice, not for the purpose of shooting NBA three-point shots, but as a reference point for where perimeter players should set up. Michigan State and Marquette have both the college and the NBA three-point lines on their practice floors.

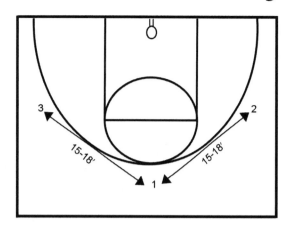

Key Offensive Statistics

It is a coach's responsibility to teach players why teams win. Too often, coaches set goals such as winning the conference championship or winning 20 games. We call these types of goals "outcome goals." We believe that it is much more important to set performance goals that describe the behavior that is necessary for a team to win.

Do your players have a clear understanding of what they need to do in order for the team to be successful? What performance goals have you set for your team? In Activity 10.1, located in the Coach's Game Plan, you will have the opportunity to establish offensive performance goals for your team.

At the University of Tennessee, Pat Summitt and her outstanding assistants Holly Warlick, Nikki Caldwell, and Dean Lockwood have established six team offensive goals for every game.

- 25 or more free throw attempts
- 75 percent or higher free throw percentage
- 50 percent or higher field goal percentage
- 15 or fewer turnovers
- 38 percent or higher three-point field goal percentage
- Outscore the opponent's bench by 15 or more points

Instant Replay

1. Two of the most important offensive factors in determining team success are making your opponent commit personal fouls and getting high-percentage shots.
2. The best way to read a post defender is through "sight and radar."
3. A "sprint to the glass mentality" is the key to successful offensive rebounding.
4. The general rule of offensive rebounding is that a team will score on 50 percent of their second-shot attempts and 80 percent of their third-shot attempts.
5. Seeing the floor involves recognition, anticipation, and execution.
6. Two keys in dribble penetration are getting past the first line of defense and then locating and beating the second-line defenders.
7. One of the biggest mistakes players make when using screens is cutting too soon. It is better to be a second late than to break early.
8. The success of the pick-and-roll depends on the ability of the screener and the ball handler to read the defense.
9. Knowing when not to shoot is just as important as knowing when to shoot.
10. Ball possession creates scoring opportunities, while turnovers are nothing more than wasted opportunities.
11. The outlet pass is the key to initiating the fast break.
12. The ideal spacing between players is 15 to 18 feet.

Coach's Game Plan

ACTIVITY 10.1 List your team's offensive performance goals for every game.

11

Defensive Keys for Team Success

My teams are built around tough defense, stingy shot selection, and being hard-nosed.

—Don Haskins, Naismith Basketball Hall of Fame Coach

Defense is the heart of the game of basketball and contributes more to winning than any other variable. When two teams of equal ability meet, the team that plays the best defense has a decided advantage. Great defenders have a defensive mind-set. They are committed to stop-

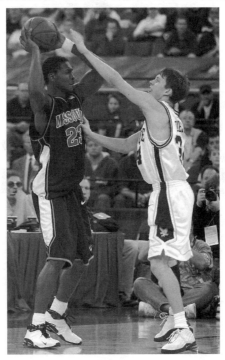

Pressure the ball. Do not allow the ball handler
a free look at the basket.

ping their opponent from scoring. They contest shots, dive for loose
balls, take charges, and attack rebounds.

Never underestimate the power of defense and rebounding. Pat
Summitt expressed it eloquently when she stated, "Offense sells tickets, defense wins games, and rebounds win championships."

At Marquette, the coaching staff believes one of the keys to winning is stopping your opponent three or more possessions in a row
because it gives the offense an opportunity to make a run. Our goal
is to make three consecutive defensive stops at least seven times during a game.

Pressure defense is the name of the game.

—Denny Crum, Naismith Basketball Hall of Fame Coach

ATTACK

Defense is both a physical and mental skill. Defenders should be encouraged to be proactive rather than reactive. Jerry Krause, director of basketball operations at Gonzaga University, and Don Meyer, coach at Northern State University, emphasize the active elements of defense with the acronym ATTACK, which stands for attitude, teamwork, tools, anticipation, concentration, and keep in the stance.

- **A—Attitude.** Defense starts with an aggressive, blue-collar attitude. Great defenders demonstrate desire, discipline, dedication, and mental toughness.
- **T—Teamwork.** The collective effort of five defenders working together is far greater than the sum of five individual efforts.
- **T—Tools.** The tools of defense are the mind, body, feet, eyes, hands, and voice.
- **A—Anticipation.** Quickness is the result of physical readiness and mental anticipation.
- **C—Concentration.** Defenders must be clearly focused on the task at hand.
- **K—Keep in the stance.** Outstanding defensive players keep their knees bent and stay in their defensive stances during the entire defensive possession.

Essentials of Defense

There is no one correct way to play defense. Every coach must formulate his or her own defensive philosophy and create a system that accomplishes those goals. Our defensive philosophy starts with the belief that good defensive teams eliminate easy baskets as much as possible. They challenge every open shot, stop dribble penetration, keep the ball out of the post area, reduce second-shot opportunities, and keep their opponent off the free throw line.

The ten essentials for reducing easy baskets are: sprint back on defense, talk on defense, pressure the ball, create deflections, stop dribble penetration, defend the pick-and-roll, contest all shots, block out, and commit no unnecessary fouls.

Individual defense is combat. It is head-to-head, hand-to-hand, and foot-to-foot.

—Ray Meyer, Naismith Basketball Hall of Fame Coach

Sprint Back on Defense

A trademark of all successful teams is transition defense, how quickly a team converts from offense to defense. Many teams play very tough defense once they are set up, but they have a difficult time getting back to set up. A big part of defense is getting from the offensive end of the court to the predetermined point of defensive attack.

It is just as important to have a good defensive transition system, as it is to have one for the offense. Many coaches neglect this area and only tell players to hustle back. When establishing a transition defensive system, coaches should consider these six factors: protecting the basket area from a long pass, pressuring the rebounder, covering the outlet pass, discouraging the sideline pass, containing the dribbler, and filling the middle of the court.

The primary rule in transition defense is to stop all fast-break layups. This is accomplished by sprinting back on defense and never being outnumbered by the offensive team. We tell our players, if the ball is ahead of you, you are in the wrong place. All defenders must race back and assume a floor position below the line of the ball. This eliminates the defensive team from being outnumbered. The first defender back must retreat to the basket area so that the defense is built from the inside out.

There will be times that the defenders will find that they are outnumbered.

In a two-on-one situation, X1's (the lone defender's) main responsibility is not to give up a layup. He or she should retreat quickly to the basket area and stay there until help arrives. The defender can use fakes to get the dribbler to pick up the ball but should never leave the basket area in an attempt to steal a pass.

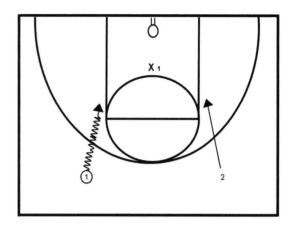

In a three-on-two situation, the two defenders sprint back into the lane and form a tandem. Communication between X1 and X2 is critical. The top defender's main responsibility is to contain the ball. The back defender, X2, protects the basket. Once the ball is passed to the wing, X1 drops back to cover the basket area. X2 breaks out under control to defend the ball and must not allow 2 to drive to the basket.

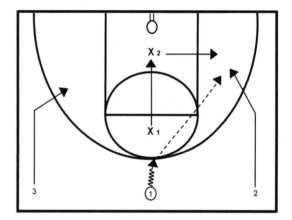

The key points in transition defense are:

- Anticipate the fast break on every possession.
- Slow down the break by pressuring the rebounder and defending the outlet man.
- Sprint back, look over the inside shoulder, and see the ball.
- Communicate with teammates.
- Do not reach wildly at the ball trying to make a steal.
- Run to a floor position below the line of the ball.
- Protect the basket area with the first player back.
- Contain the dribbler.
- Stop the ball in transition before teams can initiate early offense.

Talk on Defense

The best defensive teams have players that continually talk on defense. NBA coach Del Harris believes there has never been a great "silent defense." William "Red" Holzman, the NBA Coach of the Decade for the 1970s, had his players talking on defense all the time because he believed that "basketball is a game where the use of the mind, body, and voice are equally important." Talking on defense helped the New York Knicks win NBA titles in 1970 and 1973.

There is always action on the court that requires communication between teammates. Specific terminology should be developed so players can communicate quickly without any misunderstanding. For example, in the three-on-two situation, one defender must call out "ball." This informs his or her teammate to take the back position in the tandem and protect the basket area.

Coaches must also recognize that getting players to talk on the court is hard. So communication among players must be emphasized every practice. Key points to emphasize are:

- Always communicate with teammates when playing defense; this is the glue that holds a defense together.
- Use a common language of terms or short phrases.
- Call out all screens.
- Stay committed to communication every practice.

Pressure the Ball

The cornerstone of any defense is pressure on the ball. It doesn't make any difference whether it is man-to-man or zone, a defense cannot be effective if it allows the ball to be moved without any pressure.

Defending in a Live Ball Situation
One of the most difficult jobs of a defender is guarding a player who still has the option of dribbling. Key points when defending a live ball are:

- Stay in your defensive stance.
- Maintain balance at all times with your feet staggered, shoulder-width apart, so you can move in any direction.
- Keep the knees flexed. Never play defense with straight legs.
- Pressure the ball. Be within touching distance with the lead hand up. This hand must prevent the ball handler from bringing the ball up into the shooting pocket.
- Do not let the player have a "free look at the basket." Distort the ball handler's ability to see the floor.
- Stay between the ball and the basket, the ball-you-basket principle.
- Respect all fakes with a retreat step. A player executes the retreat step by pushing off the front foot, taking a step backward with the rear foot, and then sliding the front foot back to re-establish position and balance.
- Keep your head up and see what is going on around you by using peripheral vision.

Defending in a Dead Ball Situation

After a ball handler has picked up his or her dribble, the defensive player must attack the ball aggressively. Some coaches say "swarm" to describe this situation. A team's defense should be the most dominant in this situation.

Key points in defending a dead ball situation are:

- Yell "ball" or "dead" to heighten the defensive intensity of your teammates. They should go immediately into a full denial position.
- Trace the ball with two hands for the purpose of getting a turnover or deflection.
- Stay between the ball and the basket to eliminate an inside pass.

Create Deflections

Deflections are the barometer of aggressive defense. They reflect your players' intensity. Whenever a defender touches the ball, there is a

Attack the ball aggressively after the dribbler has picked up the dribble.

chance a teammate might steal it. Deflections create easy scoring opportunities and give the defense a decided edge in the psychological battle.

When Hubie Brown was coaching the Memphis Grizzlies, he had a goal of getting at least seven deflections in each quarter. At Marquette, the goal for every game is 35 deflections. The goal was adjusted to 40 per game in 2003 for the team that went to the Final Four, and they ended the season averaging 42 deflections per game.

In the practice gym at Marquette, a large banner lists the all-time deflection leader at each position. Entering the 2006 season, those players were Travis Diener, Dwyane Wade, Todd Townsend, Oluoma Nnamaka, and Scott Merritt. The goal for the current players is to break those records. The coaching staff also keeps a running total of deflections in practice on a laminated board, which even goes with the team on road trips. The importance of deflections is discussed every day of the season. Key points for getting deflections are:

- Keep hands and feet active.
- Mirror the ball constantly with one hand.
- Always play with the head up.
- Swarm the ball handler after the dribble is used.
- See the ball and overplay the next penetrating pass if you are the off-the-ball defender.

Stop Dribble Penetration

The key word when stopping dribble penetration is *containment.* Nothing hurts a team defense more than dribble penetration because it forces inside players to help and recover. To stop dribble penetration, a defender must maintain the proper spacing. We classify defenders into three categories. Good defensive players can defend one dribble. Very good defensive players can defend two dribbles. Superior defenders can control the ball. Key points when defending the dribbler are:

- Pressure and contain the dribbler at all times.
- Maintain a low center of gravity when the ball handler drives. Do not bob up and down as you defend the driver.
- Keep your head over the center of your body and weight evenly distributed.
- Move your feet in a step and slide sequence. Do not bring your feet together.
- Always maintain the ball-you-basket principle.
- Have active hands and feet.
- Jab and strike with the hands, but don't reach. When you reach, your feet freeze.
- Influence the ball to a designated spot.
- Always use the retreat step when the dribbler turns his or her back to you. You need to create spacing because the ball handler is trying to spin by you using a drop step.
- Make the ball handler pick up the dribble.

Keep the Ball Out of the Post Area

Post defense is the heart of defensive play. After you decide how you are going to defend the post, then you can build your defense. It is the foundation for everything you do defensively.

A post defender can play behind, in front, side-front from the high side, or side-front from the low side. There are specific situations that call for each of these defensive positions.

To be successful, the ball must be kept out of the post area. The best way to do this is either front or side-front the low post, which will also allow your perimeter defenders to stay home on outside shooters and reduce the number of personal fouls. Important points in defending the post are:

- Pressure the passer. This is the best form of post defense.
- Don't allow ball handlers on the perimeter a free look at a post player.
- Defend high post passers as if they had used their dribble. One of the most difficult passes to stop is the feed from a high post to a low post. Trace the ball so the high post cannot easily feed the low post or reverse the ball.
- Remember when defending a low post: Your feet put your hands in a position to make a play.
- Don't permit an offensive post player to get to your body and seal you.
- Don't dive or reach when the low post player catches the ball. Build a wall by establishing a position between the offensive player and the basket. Your objective is to make the post player shoot through the wall or pass the ball back outside.

Defend the Pick-and-Roll

Over the past 10 years there has been a resurgence of the pick-and-roll in college basketball. The best offensive teams in basketball today are also the best pick-and-roll teams. To beat them, you must be able to defend this play, which is a major challenge because the pick-and-roll is the most difficult play to stop in basketball.

Post defense is the heart of defensive play.

Even though there are many different defensive schemes to combat the pick-and-roll, every coach must determine his or her key tactics. Pat Summitt establishes pick-and-roll defensive concepts during the first month of every season. She installs a standard defense consisting of the following key points:

- The defender on the ball handler must force the dribbler to use the screen. Do not give the ball handler an option.
- The screener's defender must step out aggressively and "show his or her numbers" to the dribbler using the screen. This tactic is called a "heavy hedge" and is similar to a fake trap. For a split second, many people will think that you are trapping the ball handler.
- Once the dribbler's defender gets back in front of the ball, the screener's defender recovers.
- If the screener slips the pick, the defender guarding the screener must go also. The teaching point is for the defender to "keep a hand on the back" of the screener. This enables the defender to know exactly where the screener is at all times.

Defenses must contest every shot.

Contest All Shots

A defender must challenge all shots. This lowers opponents' shooting percentages and increases a team's chances of winning. The key teaching points when contesting a shot are:

- Don't leave the floor until the shooter does.
- Fully extend the lead arm and make yourself as tall as you can be.
- Keep the lead hand in a vertical position with the wrist back. Do not swat at the shot.
- Apply verbal pressure by shouting "shot."

Block Out

Winning basketball teams do not allow their opponents second-shot opportunities. They keep offensive rebounders from securing rebounds by blocking out and maintaining the inside rebounding position. Hall of Fame coach Chuck Daly believes that blocking out is the single most difficult thing to sell to your players.

Successful rebounding requires all five defensive players to block out and attack the boards. Guards play a key role in defensive rebounding. In 2006, Marquette's freshmen guards 5'11" Dominic James and 6'3" Jerel McNeal combined for nine rebounds per game.

The most important principle in rebounding is to play every shot as if it will be missed. Great rebounders are relentless and always make the second and third effort. Defenders must be aware of when and where a shot is taken and remember that the longer the shot, the longer the rebound. Plus, a missed shot from the wing or corner will be rebounded on the weak side approximately 70 percent of the time.

After the shot goes up, all defenders must locate the opponent they are responsible for blocking out or the opposing player nearest to them. This sets the stage for the actual block out.

Blocking out requires either a front pivot or a rear pivot, which enables the defenders to make contact with their bodies rather than just their arms. Their feet are parallel and shoulder-width apart, and their arms are raised and bent at the elbows with the hands up.

The period of time between the release of the shot and the point when the ball can be rebounded is crucial. Teaching players when to release the block out and go after the ball is one of the most important teaching points in rebounding. We emphasize to our players not to hold the block out too long.

As a coach, it is important to realize what type of rebounders you have on your team. Occasionally you will have a player we call a "range rebounder." These athletes can go out of their area and retrieve rebounds and do not have to be great block out players. Most of the time, however, your players must block out and get their opponent on their back.

Key points in blocking out are:

- Assume every shot will be missed.
- Get position. All five defensive players must block out.

Block out and then go after the missed shot.

- Be aware of when and where a shot is taken.
- Always block out the shooter, as he or she is the most dangerous rebounder.
- Make contact with your opponent using either a front or rear pivot.
- Keep your body between your opponent and the basket, and follow the flight of the ball.
- Don't hold the block out too long.
- Go to the boards with your hands up.
- Don't jump until you see where the ball is going.
- Secure the rebound with two hands and quickly bring it to the "chin it" position. Ball control is essential.

Do Not Commit Unnecessary Fouls

While defense must be played aggressively, special emphasis must be placed on not fouling. Excellent defensive teams demonstrate great discipline in being able to pressure the ball without putting their opponents on the free throw line.

Players who are not in the proper stance or defensive floor position commit the majority of fouls. Common examples are when defenders fail to adjust their floor positions when the ball is passed or when their players move. This often results in foolish fouls such as reaching in or holding. It may also force teammates to foul because they are covering for the defender who was in the wrong position. Six critical areas that often result in personal fouls are: early transition, second-shot opportunities, post defense, defending screens, guarding a dribbler, and contesting a shot.

There are two cardinal rules when it comes to personal fouls.

1. Don't commit fouls that could result in a three-point play. Players are expected to contest every shot the opponent takes without fouling.
2. Don't commit foolish fouls. Always be aware of time, score, and situation. You should not foul a player 40 feet from the basket unless it is a late-game strategy. Never foul at the end of the shot clock because it sabotages all the hard work your team has done.

Key Defensive Statistics

Do your players have a clear understanding of what they need to do defensively in order for the team to be successful? What defensive performance goals have you set for your team? In Activity 11.1 of the Coach's Game Plan at the end of this chapter, you will have the opportunity to establish defensive performance goals for your team.

At the University of Tennessee, the Lady Vols coaches have established five defensive goals for every game.

- No transition layups
- 30 or more deflections
- 12 or more steals
- 20 or more forced turnovers
- 15 or fewer free throw attempts

If you play good, hard defense, the offense will take care of itself.

—William "Red" Holzman, Naismith Basketball Hall of Fame Coach

---

Instant Replay

1. Defense is the heart of the game of basketball and contributes more to winning than any other variable.
2. The best defensive teams have players that continually talk on defense.
3. The cornerstone of any defense is pressure on the ball.
4. Deflections are the barometer of aggressive defense.
5. Containment is the key to stopping dribble penetration.
6. Players helping off the ball must stop dribble penetration.
7. A defender must challenge and contest all shots.
8. The most important principle in rebounding is to play every shot as if it will be missed.
9. The shooter is the most dangerous rebounder and must be blocked out.
10. Don't commit personal fouls that could result in three-point plays.
11. The best form of post defense is to pressure the passer.
12. When defending a low post, your feet put your hands in a position to make a play.

Coach's Game Plan

ACTIVITY 11.1 List your team's defensive performance goals for every game.

12
Winning Plays

On offense, a successful team must adhere to the principles of spacing, shot selection, and handling the ball.

—Bob Knight, Naismith Basketball Hall of Fame Coach

All successful coaches have designated plays within their offensive systems. They constantly search for new plays to better utilize their talent and outmaneuver the multiple defenses of their opponents. This chapter includes baseline out-of-bounds plays, sideline out-of-bounds plays, and half-court offensive plays.

Baseline Out-of-Bounds Plays

There are two primary objectives in any baseline out-of-bounds play. The first is to keep possession of the ball after the pass-in. The play should be designed so the ball is brought safely inbounds within the five-second time limit. In order for this to occur, the inbounds passer must designate the play to his or her teammates prior to receiving the ball from the official. This will provide time for all players to get to their predetermined positions. After the players reach their correct starting spots, the play begins on a signal by the inbounds passer. Various signals can be used to start the movement of the players, including slapping the ball, raising the ball over the head, dropping the ball in a quick dribble, or orally calling out a name or number.

The second objective is to get the ball to an offensive player in a high-percentage shooting area. The specific plays should be designed to take advantage of the available players and provide secondary options in case the defense takes away the first option. All inbounds plays should make available a safety outlet so that a team can maintain possession even if the primary scoring opportunities are taken away. The success of baseline out-of-bounds plays depends on perfect timing and proper execution. As used here, the acronym BOB stands for *baseline out-of-bounds play*.

BOB Play #1

- **1** cuts to the weak side corner.
- **5** breaks off **1** to the strong side.
- **3** passes to **5** and loops to the perimeter.

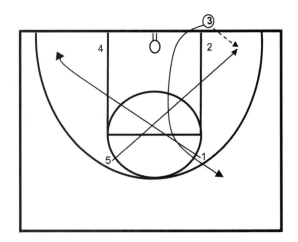

- **5** looks for an inside feed to **2**.
- **4** flashes to the high post.
- **1** spots up at the three-point line on the weak side.

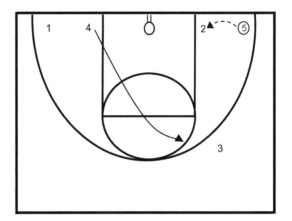

- **5** passes to **4**.
- **2** sets a back screen for a shuffle cut for **5**.
- **4** can pass to **5** in the lane, reverse the ball to **1** for a shot, or pass inside to **5**.

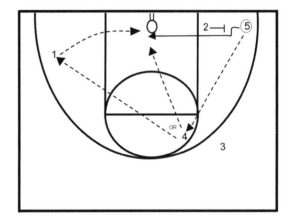

- If the pass cannot be made to **4** on the flash cut, **5** passes to **3**.
- **5** then screens for **2** for a shot or a post feed back to **5**.

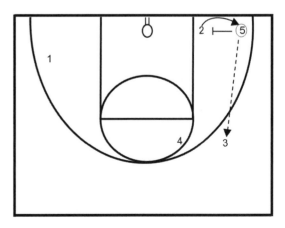

BOB Play #2

- **1** and **5** set staggered screens for **2** who cuts hard to the wing.
- **5** rolls back into the lane looking for a lob pass.
- **4** steps into the lane looking for a pass from **3**.

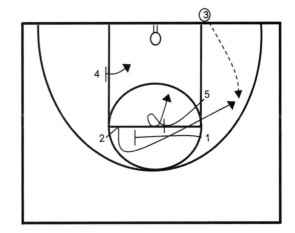

- If **2** doesn't take the shot, **5** posts up looking for the pass from **2**.
- **3** receives a double screen from **4** and **1**.

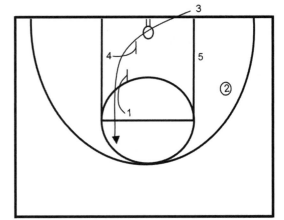

BOB Play #3

- **4** breaks to the corner for the inbounds pass.
- At the same time, **5** screens diagonally for **3** for a perimeter shot.
- If the defense switches, **5** posts up in the lane against the mismatch.

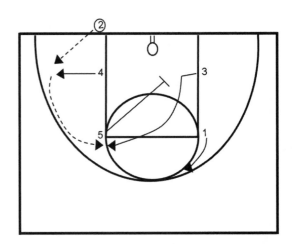

- If **3** does not have the shot, **4** screens for **2** for a possible shot.
- If **3** does not pass to **2**, **5** screens **4**'s defender and **4** cuts into the lane over the top of the screen looking for the ball.
- **5**'s defender may help on **4**, which makes **5** a primary receiver in the low post.

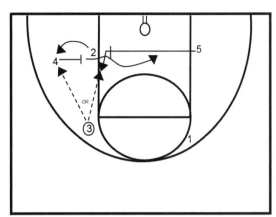

BOB Play #4

- **2** sets a back screen for **3**, who cuts hard to the basket looking for a pass and a layup.
- After setting the screen, **2** cuts off **4** and **5**, who have set staggered screens.
- After setting the last screen, **5** slips to the basket and may be open if his or her defender helps on **2**.

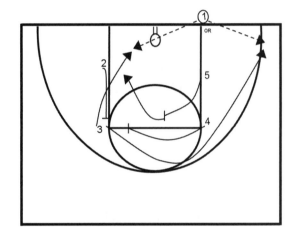

BOB Play #5

- **2** breaks to the corner and receives the pass from **3**.
- **5** screens for **1**. **2** passes to **1**, and **3** steps into the post.

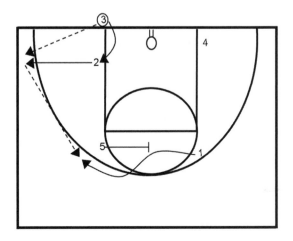

- **2** cuts off staggered screens by **3**, **4**, and **5**.
- **1** looks for a quick post-up by **3** or a pass to **2** for the jump shot.

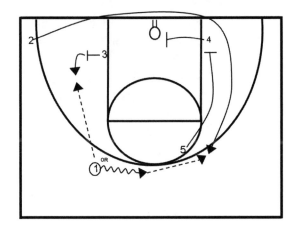

BOB Play #6

- This play is designed for situations when there is only one second remaining on the clock.
- Players **5**, **4**, and **3** are positioned in a tight line, with **3** setting up near the elbow.
- **5** makes an outside cut off players **4** and **3** and then cuts hard to the basket looking for a lob pass.
- As soon as **5** breaks to the basket, **3** cuts to the corner for a possible jump shot.

BOB Play #7

- **5** screens for **2**, who cuts to the wing for the pass from **3**.
- **5** sets a screen for **3**, who breaks up the lane and looks for the perimeter shot.

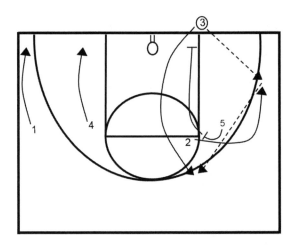

- **1**, **4**, **5**, and **2** flatten out to the baseline, setting up a low **1–4** alignment.
- **3** has the opportunity to penetrate and create a scoring play.

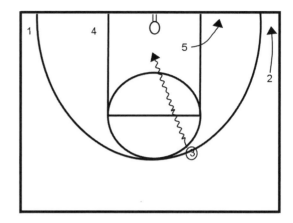

BOB Play #8

- **1** breaks out to the corner for the pass from **2**.
- **2** cuts to the point using the triple staggered screens set by **3**, **4**, and **5**.
- **1** passes to **2** for a three-point shot attempt.

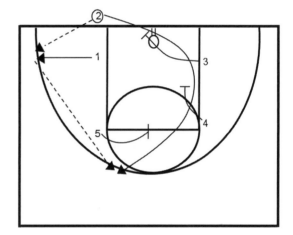

BOB Play #9

- **5** screens diagonally in the middle of the lane for **1**.
- **4** turns and screens **5**'s defender.
- **5** rolls to the basket looking for the pass.
- **4** reverse pivots to the basket and will be open if there is a defensive switch.

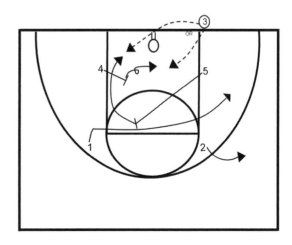

BOB Play #10

- **5** breaks out for the pass from **3**.
- The ball is reversed to **1** and then to **4**.
- After **2** screens down for **4**, **3** back screens for **5**.
- **4** throws a lob pass to **5**.

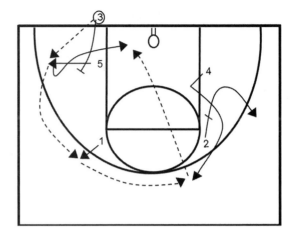

- If the lob pass is not thrown to **5**, **4** reverses the ball to **2**.
- **2** looks inside for **5**.
- **1** and **4** screen down for **3**, who looks for the perimeter shot.

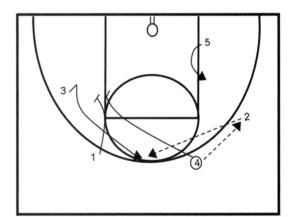

- If **3** catches the ball at the top of the circle but is unable to shoot, **5** flashes to the free throw line and **2** breaks backdoor.
- **3** can also look to the weak side as **4** screens for **1**.
- **1** can either shoot or feed the ball inside to **4**.

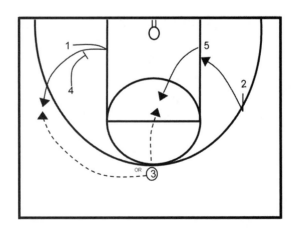

Sideline Out-of-Bounds Plays

Basketball coaches are continually looking for ways to enhance their offensive output, and one area sometimes overlooked is sideline out-of-bounds plays. If coaches reviewed game statistics, they would find that between four and six times per game, the ball was awarded to them in their front court on the sideline. Training your players to take advantage of these situations could help your team score an additional 8–12 points.

Many teams do not attain good results from their sideline out-of-bounds plays because they either have not spent enough time perfecting them or they have not practiced them under gamelike conditions. Players have a tendency to become very lackluster when practicing out-of-bounds plays, and coaches must demand concentration and perfect execution. Five minutes of each practice session should be devoted to this phase of the game, and the plays should be rehearsed against various types of defenses. One way to do this is to incorporate your out-of-bounds plays in your half-court and full-court controlled scrimmages.

The following factors must be considered when deciding which sideline out-of-bounds play should be run:

- The score of the game
- The time remaining
- The type and aggressiveness of the defense
- The out-of-bounds spot from where the ball is being thrown in

Here, SOB stands for *sideline out-of-bounds play*.

SOB Play #1

- **2** screens for **1**, while **5** cuts from the opposite block to quickly screen for **2**.
- **3** looks to throw the lob pass to **2**.
- **4** steps toward the ball as a safety release.

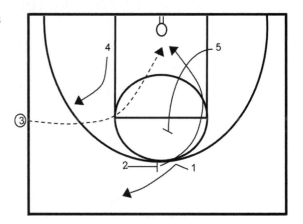

SOB Play #2

- **5** flashes and receives a pass from **3**.
- **3** follows the pass and receives a quick return pass from **5**.
- **3** looks to drive to the basket or pull up for a perimeter shot.

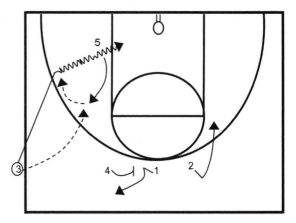

SOB Play #3

- **1** breaks out of the line for the pass from **3**.
- At the same time, **2** begins to cut to the baseline.
- **5** cuts into the lane to set the first screen for **2**.
- **3** cuts inside of **4** and sets the second screen for **2**.
- **4** circles out toward the left wing and will set the third screen for **2**.
- **1** passes to **2** coming off the three staggered screens.

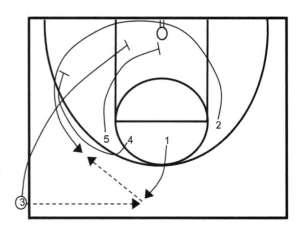

SOB Play #4

- **2** breaks to the point and receives the inbounds pass from **3**.
- **3** breaks off **1** and goes to the weak side wing.
- **1** breaks to the strong side wing and receives the pass from **2**.

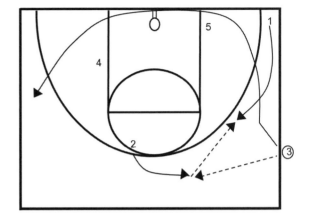

- The primary purpose of this play is to get the ball inside to **5**.
- **1** feeds the post player **5** and sets a high screen for **2** and a down screen for **4**.
- **5** looks to shoot or pass to **2** or **4** cutting off screens.

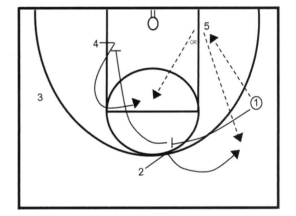

SOB Play #5

- **2** moves down the lane trying to make his or her defender think it is a back cut to the basket.
- **2** then uses the screen set by **5** and breaks toward the corner looking for the pass and shot.
- At the same time that **2** is attempting to get open, **1** sets a back pick for **4. 4** breaks to the basket looking for a possible lob pass. If the lob pass is not thrown, **4** assumes a weak side rebounding position.

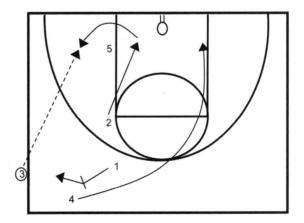

- If **2** receives the pass, **5** steps out and sets a screen for **2**, creating a pick-and-roll option.

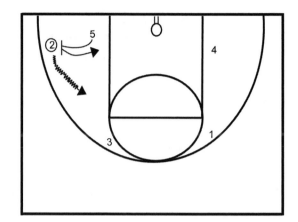

- If the defense is very aggressive and denies the pass to **2** in the corner, **5** breaks hard to the ball looking for the pass.
- **2** breaks to the basketball on a backdoor cut.

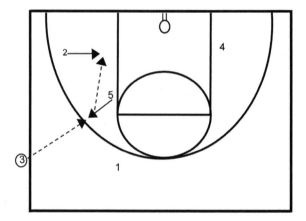

- Against a zone defense, the first look is to **2** breaking to the corner.
- If the entry pass cannot be made to **2**, the ball is inbounded to **1**.
- **5** and **4** screen the back line defenders of the zone.
- **2** cuts across the lane looking for a pass from **1**.

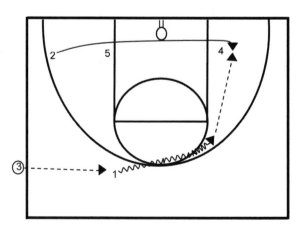

Half-Court Offense

Winning basketball coaches create offenses designed to maximize the strengths of their players. This section includes eight half-court plays that have been used successfully at Marquette.

Marquette Play #1

- **1** dribbles to the wing at the same time **4** down screens for **2**.
- **2** zipper cuts off **4**'s screen and receives the pass from **1**. **2** must pivot and get in the triple-threat position quickly.
- On the weak side, **5** down screens for **3**. **5** must plant and pivot in preparation for the post-up.

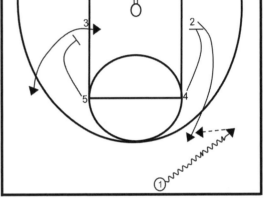

- **2** passes to **3** at the wing and then screens down for **4**.

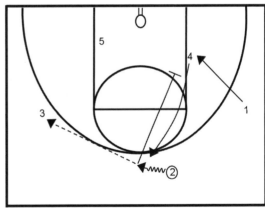

- **3** passes to **4** at the top of the circle.
- **1** inverts with **2** and sets a cross screen for **5**.
- **4** swings the ball to **2**.
- **5** must reverse pivot off the cross screen.

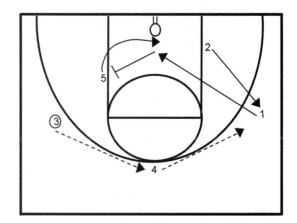

- If **2** does not pass to **5**, **4** sets a down screen for **1**.
- **2** passes to **1** at the top of the circle.

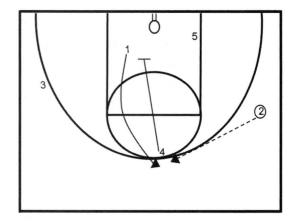

Marquette Play #2

- **2** pops to the wing.
- **1** passes to **2**.

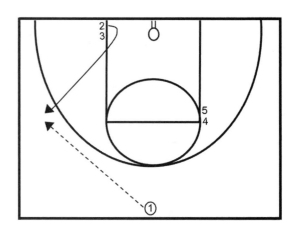

- **3** sets a screen at the elbow.
- **1** fakes using **3**'s screen, but instead, **1** sets a ball screen for **2**.
- **3** makes a flare cut off **5** and **4**.
- **5** cuts to the basket and **4** pops out.

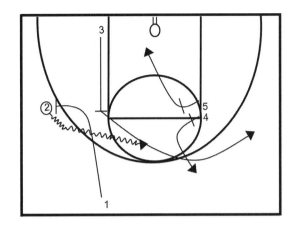

Marquette Play #3

- **3** pops to the wing.
- **1** passes to **3** and then **3** returns the pass to **1**.
- **5** sets a ball screen for **1**.
- **2** breaks out to the wing as **1** uses **5**'s screen.

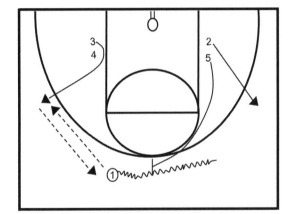

- **3** cuts to the corner off **5**.
- **5** screens for **4**.
- **1** passes to **4**.

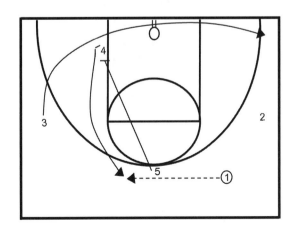

- **4** dribbles to the wing.
- **4** passes to **5** on the post-up.

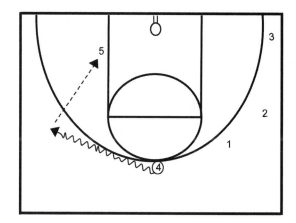

Marquette Play #4

- **2** cuts over **5**.
- **1** dribbles at **2**.
- **3** cuts off the screen by **4**.
- **1** passes to **3**.

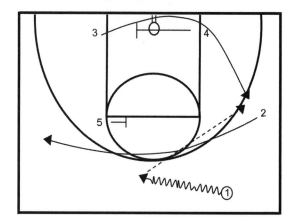

Marquette Play #5

- **1** passes to **5**.
- **1** and **2** loop.
- **4** screens for **1**; **3** screens for **2**.

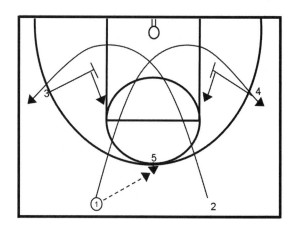

- **5** passes to **2**.
- **3** sets a cross screen for **4**.
- **3** comes off the down screen set by **5**, looking for an open shot.

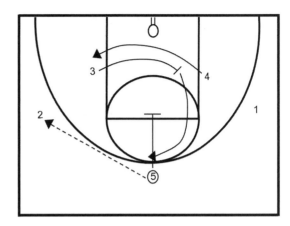

Marquette Play #6

- **1** sets a cross screen for **2** and then loops back toward the corner.
- **2** uses the screen and breaks out to the wing.
- **3** passes to **2**.
- **4** sets a back screen for **3**.
- **2** looks for the lob pass to **3**.

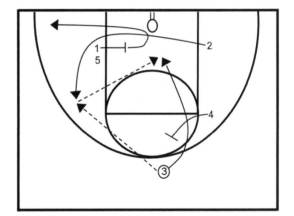

- If the lob pass is not open, **2** passes to **4**.
- **3** and **5** break out outside to open up the middle of the court.
- **2** breaks off **4**, receives the handoff, and looks to drive to the basket.

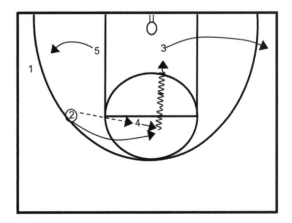

Marquette Play #7

- **3** breaks out to the wing and receives the pass from **1**.
- **1** cuts to the corner.
- **3** looks inside for a possible pass to **5**.
- If **5** is defended on the high side, **3** passes to **1**.
- **1** feeds **5**.

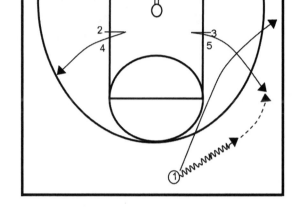

- If **5** is defended on the low side, **4** makes a flash cut to the elbow.
- **3** passes to **4**.
- **4** feeds **5**.

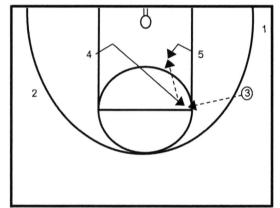

Marquette Play #8

- **5** sets a high ball screen for **1**.
- **2** breaks across the lane and sets a cross screen for **4**.
- **1** uses **5**'s screen and looks for a quick feed to **4**.

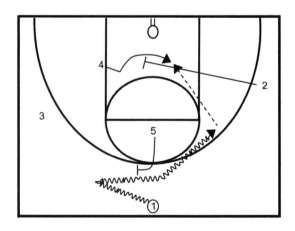

- **5** sets a down screen for **2**.
- **2** uses the screen and looks for the pass from **1**.

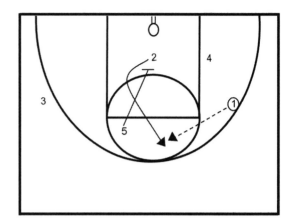

- As a variation of the previous play, **5** and **3** can set a double screen or a staggered screen for **2**.
- **2** receives the pass from **1** and looks for the open shot or pass inside.

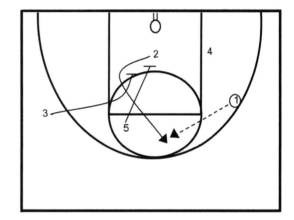

Instant Replay

1. At least five minutes of every practice should be devoted to perfecting out-of-bounds plays.
2. Out-of-bounds plays should be practiced under gamelike conditions.
3. The primary objective in any out-of-bounds play is to get the ball safely inbounds within the five-second time limit.
4. The second objective in any out-of-bounds play is to get the ball to an offensive player in a position on the court that increases the team's opportunity to score.
5. Half-court offenses should be designed to maximize the strengths of the players and create high percentage shots on every possession.

Afterword

Teamwork is the most important factor in determining basketball success on every level of the game. The 2006 NBA Playoffs confirmed this fact and reinforced the principles presented in this book.

The Miami Heat shocked the basketball world by winning the NBA championship with a team composed of players who most basketball experts thought would implode because of poor team chemistry. Basketball fans throughout the world marveled at Miami's accomplishments and wondered how this could happen. The authors contend that this is the perfect present-day example of getting 15 individuals to play as one committed unit.

Part 2 of *Coaching Team Basketball* provided a blueprint for team play emphasizing strong leadership, core values, visionary thinking, talented team players, and team unity. Coach Pat Riley masterfully applied these principles in such a way that the 2006 version of the Miami Heat earned a permanent place in NBA history.

There are few individuals as focused and competitive as Pat Riley. He pulled out all the stops during a tremulous season. Riley convinced his cadre of Shaquille O'Neal, Gary Payton, Antoine Walker, and Alonzo Mourning that the real measure of greatness wasn't what a player can do by himself, but how much better he makes those around him. He told them if they played together and stayed strong, they would be champions.

The players bought into Riley's core values and the end product was trust among a corps of unlikely teammates. The players took ownership of Riley's motto "15 Strong" and refused to buckle during adverse times. After losing the first two games of the NBA Finals to Dallas, almost everyone had written them off. But the Heat stormed back and won the next four games because they stayed together and never gave up. The Miami Heat players never stopped believing.

"We have a faith-based team here," said Riley. "A lot of people don't understand what that means. You must have faith in each other and believe in what you are doing in order to summon the courage and perseverance that it takes to be a champion."

"This team was built for the playoffs," said Dwyane Wade. "Not at one moment did one of us not believe in each other. That's what the playoffs are about, guys coming in and stepping up. It's team basketball, man."

No talk about the Miami Heat's season would be complete without discussing the beauty of Dwyane Wade. Wade's rise to stardom is a magnificent story. As a youngster growing up in Chicago, he watched all the Bulls games on television and was enthralled with Michael Jordan. Dwyane studied Jordan's tapes and even took notes as he watched Michael play. In fact, part of Wade's preparation before every game in grade school was to watch *Come Fly with Me*, a 40-minute tape of spectacular highlights from Jordan's college and professional career.

"I remember when Jordan did his famous shot," said Wade. "I went right in the backyard to see if I could do it myself. Even though I was young and really had no athletic ability, every time I saw my favorite players—Jordan and Scottie Pippen—do anything; I tried to imitate it and act like I was part of the team. I've been a big dreamer, and I'm going to continue to be a big dreamer."

Dwyane has spent his entire life meeting challenges that many thought were insurmountable. He succeeds because of his uncommon drive to excel. The more someone doubts him, the more he gets it done. In the NBA Playoffs, Miami's opponents dared Wade to take perimeter shots because they did not think he could make enough to beat them. Dwyane responded by making more three-pointers than he had in the entire regular season.

The player they call "D-Wade" and "Flash" can make taking over a game look effortless. In the NBA Finals, when the game was on the line in the fourth quarter, Dwyane averaged almost 10 points. In Game six, Wade did not score his first basket until there was only 1:59 left in the first quarter. By the end of the quarter, Wade had scored 7 points and cut the Dallas lead to 7. In the second quarter, Dwyane hit a jump shot that started Miami's rally back from an 11-point deficit. Then in the third quarter, with the game tied, Wade blocked a lay-up that sparked a 6-0 Miami spurt. And late in the fourth quarter, with Miami holding on to only a 3-point lead, Wade found James Posey wide open for a 3-point shot. For the game, Dwyane had 36 points, 10 rebounds, five assists, four steals, and three blocks.

Like soldiers in the U.S. Army Special Forces who respectfully are referred to as "quiet professionals" because of their unwavering drive and commitment to complete missions selflessly, Dwyane Wade is the epitome of the "quiet professional" in the game of basketball. He is relentless in his pursuit of team goals and does not let individual stardom affect who he is. Dwyane stays close to his roots and displays gratitude for all the wonderful things that have happened in his life. He praises teammates as "guys I grew up admiring." He credits everyone who helped, including family, teachers, and coaches.

Dwyane actively supports efforts to help underprivileged children and truly believes that "kids are our future."

As we look ahead, many lessons can be learned from stars such as Dwyane Wade. He keeps his family and his values at the forefront of everything he does. He is self-assured and never negatively responds to people's lack of confidence in him or their enormous expectations. When the game is on the line, you want the ball in his hands. Dwyane is one of those special people who think big, but focus small.

Glossary

Assist A pass from an offensive player to a teammate that results in an immediate score.

Backboard The rounded or rectangular board placed behind the basket.

Backcourt That half of the court that is the farthest from the offensive basket; also, the position played by the guards.

Backdoor cut A cut behind the defender toward the basket against a defensive overplay.

Back screen A move by an offensive player away from the basket to set a screen for a teammate.

Ball screen A screen on the defender guarding the offensive player with the ball.

Ball side The side of the court on which the ball is located; also called the *strong side.*

Bank shot A shot in which the ball strikes the backboard and then rebounds into the basket.

Baseline The out-of-bounds line underneath either basket on both ends of the floor.

Basket A goal that results in a score; also, the rim through which the ball is thrown.

Block out A rebounding position with the rebounder making contact and staying between the basket and the opponent.

Bounce pass A pass that hits the floor between the passer and the receiver.

Catch and face A technique for receiving a pass and squaring up to the basket in the triple-threat position.

Center Often the tallest player on a team; normally plays close to the basket and is responsible for securing rebounds and blocking shots.

Chin it The position of the ball after a rebound; the player holds the ball directly under the chin with the elbows and fingers up.

Clear out When an offensive player leaves an area so the ball handler has more room to maneuver.

Cross screen A lateral move by an offensive player to set a screen for a teammate.

Cut An offensive move used to create an advantage; it is usually made toward the basket, the ball, or a teammate.

Defense The act of attempting to prevent your opponent from scoring.

Down screen A move by an offensive player toward the baseline to set a screen for a teammate.

Dribble drive Dribbling in a straight line to the basket.

Dribbler An offensive player that moves the ball on the court by legally bouncing it with one hand.

Early offense A secondary break situation when the fast break is not available but the defense is not yet set.

Elbow The area of the court where the free throw line and the free throw lane line intersect.

Endline Also referred to as the *baseline*.

Fake A technique used to get a defensive player off balance or out of position.

Fast break An offensive tactic in which a team rapidly moves the ball the length of the court by long passes and/or quick dribble drives in an attempt to score before the opponent can set up its defense.

Field goal A basket made while the ball is in play.

Field goal percentage The percentage of converted field goal attempts.

Forwards Two players generally positioned closer to the basket than the guards; they often assume a floor position along the perimeters of the free throw lane and maneuver both inside and outside.

Free throw An unguarded attempt to score from a line 15 feet from the basket.

Free throw percentage The percentage of converted free throw attempts.

Frontcourt The offensive area of the court from the midcourt line to the baseline; also, the positions played by the forwards and center.

Front pivot Moving forward while turning on the pivot foot.

Give-and-go An offensive maneuver whereby a player passes to a teammate and cuts for the basket looking for a return pass; sometimes called an *inside cut*.

Guards The two players who typically move the ball from the backcourt into the frontcourt and then position themselves farthest from the basket.

Help side The side of the court opposite that of the ball; also called the *weak side*.

High post An area of the court located near the free throw line.

Inside cut When the offensive player passes the ball to a teammate and cuts to the basket looking for a return pass.

Jab step A small step toward the defensive player with the nonpivot foot.

Jump shot An offensive shot in which the offensive player's feet leave the floor.

Jump stop Coming to a full stop by jumping off one foot and landing in a parallel or a staggered stance with both feet hitting the floor at the same time; also called a *quick stop*.

Layup shot A close-in shot made when moving to the basket.

Low post An area of the court located near the basket.

Midcourt line The line in the middle of the court that separates the frontcourt from the backcourt; also called the *ten-second line*.

Offense The team that has possession of the ball.

Outlet pass A pass made from a rebounder to an offensive teammate.

Paint The area inside the free throw lane.

Passing lane The area between two offensive players where a pass can be made.

Penetrate and pitch Action where the dribbler drives toward the goal and, if stopped by another defender, passes to a teammate for an open shot.

Penetration When the ball is dribbled or passed inside the defensive area toward the basket.

Pick A screen set by an offensive player.

Pick-and-roll When an offensive player screens for the ball handler and then rolls toward the basket; designed to make the defense switch or help, enabling one of the offensive players involved to have a scoring opportunity.

Pivot The rotation of the body around one foot that is kept in a stationary position.

Point guard Usually a team's floor leader who initiates the offense and controls the tempo of the game.

Post area The area around the free throw lane.

Post player The position usually played by the center.

Post-up An offensive position close to and facing away from the basket in preparation to receive a pass.

Power layup shot A layup used when closely guarded.

Ready position Stance with the knees bent, the hands up and ready, and the head up and looking forward.

Rear pivot Stepping backward while turning on the pivot foot; sometimes called a *reverse pivot*.

Rebound Securing the ball off the backboard or the rim after a missed shot attempt.

Reverse pivot Also referred to as a *rear pivot*.

Screen An offensive technique used to block or delay an opponent from reaching a desired floor position.

Screen-and-roll Also referred to as a *pick-and-roll*.

Seal When an offensive player uses his body to prevent the defensive player from denying him the ball.

Second shots Offensive shot taken after gaining an offensive rebound.

Shooting guard Generally, the player who takes the majority of the shots from the perimeter, many of which are three-point attempts.

Shooting pocket The area of the body under a player's dominant shoulder where a shot is initiated; it is the triple-threat ball position.

Skip pass Cross-court pass over the weak side defense.

Small forward Usually bigger than the guards but smaller than the power forward; responsibilities include both inside and outside work.

Spacing Refers to the optimum distance on the perimeter for establishing passing angles and driving lanes by having the offensive players 15 to 18 feet apart to make defensive double-teaming and helping difficult.

Switch A defensive tactic of changing the offensive players being guarded by the defenders for the purpose of taking something away from the offense.

Three-point shot A field goal attempt from outside the three-point line.

Transition Changing from defense to offense and vice versa.

Trap A defensive tactic in which two players double-team the ball handler.

Triple-threat position An offensive position from which the ball handler can either shoot, pass, or dribble.

Turnover An error or mistake that causes the offensive team to lose possession of the ball.

UCLA cut A passer's vertical cut from the top of the high post to the baseline following his or her pass to the wing.

"V" cut A fake in one direction and movement in the opposite direction in order to get open for a pass.

Weak side Also referred to as the *help side*.

Wing A perimeter position on the side of the basket outside the free throw line.

References

Adams, Rick. *Teams That Win*. Kearney, NE: Morris Publishing, 2001.

Allen, Nate, and Tony Burgess. *Taking the Guidon*. Published by the Center for Company-Level Leadership, Delaware, 2001.

Bembry, Jerry. "Audible: Kevin Garnett." *ESPN The Magazine*. (2005, November 7.)

Bilas, Jay. "NBA Reach Has Changed College Coaching." http://proxy.espn.go.com/ncb/columns/story?columnist= bilas_jay&id=1940454. (2004, December 7.)

Billick, Brian, with James A. Peterson. *Competitive Leadership*. Chicago: Triumph Books, 2001.

Brown, Herb. *Let's Talk Defense*. New York: McGraw-Hill, 2005.

Clarke, Bruce. *Field Manual 25-101 Battle Focused Training*. Washington D.C.: Department of the Army, 1990.

Covey, Stephen, Roger Merrill, and Rebecca Merrill. *First Things First*. New York: Simon & Schuster, 1994.

Donnithorne, Larry. *The West Point Way of Leadership*. New York: Doubleday, 1993.

Emerson, Ralph Waldo. *Selected Writings of Ralph Waldo Emerson*. New York: Penguin Group, 1965.

Feigen, Jonathan. "Pistons Create a Model Worth Duplicating." *Houston Chronicle*. (2004, June 17.)

Franschilla, Fran. "Changes Need to Happen Across Basketball." http://proxy.espn.go.com/oly/summer04/basketball/columns/ story?id=1869953. (2004, August 28.)

Harris, Del. *Winning Defense*. Indianapolis, IN: Masters Press, 1993.

Hayes, Woody. *You Win with People*. Columbus: Typographic Printing Co, 1973.

Headquarters, Department of the Army. *SH 21–76, Ranger Handbook*. Fort Benning, GA.: United States Army Infantry School, 2000.

Headquarters, Department of the Army. *Field Manual (FM) 22–100, Military Leadership*. Washington DC: Department of the Army, 1999.

Headquarters, Department of the Army. *Field Manual (FM) 25–101, Training the Force: Battle Focused Training*. Washington DC: Department of the Army, 1990.

Hill, Andrew, with John Wooden. *Be Quick: But Don't Hurry!* New York: Simon and Schuster, 2001.

Holtz, Lou. *Winning Every Day*. New York: HarperCollins, 1998.

Jackson, Phil, and Hugh Delehanty. *Sacred Hoops*. New York: Hyperion, 1995.

Knight, Bob, and Pete Newell. *Basketball According to Knight and Newell*, vol. 1. Seymour, IN: Graessler-Mercer, 1986.

Krause, Jerry, Don Meyer, and Jerry Meyer. *Basketball Skills and Drills*. Champaign, IL: Human Kinetics, 1999.

Krause, Jerry, and Ralph Pim. *Basketball Defense*. Monterey, CA: Coaches Choice, 2005.

Krause, Jerry, and Ralph Pim. *Basketball Offense*. Monterey, CA: Coaches Choice, 2005.

Krause, Jerry, and Ralph Pim. *Beyond the Xs and Os*. Monterey, CA: Coaches Choice, 2006.

Krzyzewski, Mike, with Donald Phillips. *Leading with the Heart*. New York: Warner Books, 2000.

Lavin, James. *Management Secrets of the New England Patriots*, vol. 2. Stamford, CT: Pointer Press, 2005.

Le Batard, Dan. "All That." *ESPN The Magazine*. (2005, October 10.)

McClellan, Michael D. *The Godfather*. http:Celtic-Nation.com. (2002, August 28.)

Meyer, John G. *Company Command*. Alexandria, VA: Byrrd Enterprises, 1994.

Paterno, Joe. *Paterno: By the Book*. New York: Random House, 1989.

Pim, Ralph. *Winning Basketball*. New York: McGraw-Hill, 2004.

Pitino, Rick, with Bill Reynolds. *Success Is a Choice*. New York: Broadway Books, 1997.

Riley, Pat. *The Winner Within*. New York: Putnam, 1993.

Robertson, Oscar. "Putting the 'I' in the Lakers." *New York Times*. (February 18, 2006.)

Russell, Bill, with David Falkner. *Russell Rules*. New York: Penguin Group, 2001.

Smith, Dean, John Kilgo, and Sally Jenkins. *A Coach's Life*. New York: Random House, 2002.

Smith, Dean, and Gerald D. Bell with John Kilgo. *The Carolina Way*. New York: Penguin Press, 2004.

Snair, Scott. *West Point Leadership Lessons*. Naperville, IL: Sourcebooks, 2004.

Sokolove, Michael. "Clang!" *New York Times Magazine*. (2005, February 13.)

Stark, Douglas. *Showtime*. Naismith Memorial Basketball Hall of Fame Enshrinement Program, 2002.

Summitt, Pat, with Sally Jenkins. *Reach for the Summitt*. New York: Broadway Books, 1998.

Warrior Ethos. http://www.tradoc.army.mil/pao/Web_specials/Warrior Ethos.

Williams, Pat. *Go for the Magic*. Nashville: Thomas Nelson Publishers, 1995.

Williams, Pat. *The Magic of Teamwork*. Nashville: Thomas Nelson Publishers, 1997.

Williams, Pat, with Michael Weinreb. *How to Be Like Mike*. Deerfield Beach, FL: Health Communications, 2001.

Wilstein, Steve. "Playing the Right Way Brings Gold to U.S. Women: Men's Hoops Could Have Learned from their Female Counterparts." http://msnbc.msn.com/id/5851871, 2004

Wise, Mike. "We Got No Game: Poor Fundamentals Cost Americans a Shot at the Gold." *Washington Post*. (2004, August 28.)

Wooden, John, with Steve Jamison. *Wooden*. Lincolnwood, IL: Contemporary Books, 1997.

Wooden, John, with Jack Tobin. *They Call Me Coach*. Chicago: Contemporary Books, 1998.

Index

Acronyms, 11, 68, 153
Advice for young coaches, 45
Agility, 92
American versus foreign players, 6–7
Anderson, Dave, 12
Assistant coaches, 94–96
Assists, 123, 125
ATTACK, 153
Auerbach, Red, 48–49, 99

Baker, John, 66
Barro, Ousmane, 84–85
Barry, Rick, 100
Baseline out-of-bounds plays, 168–74
Bee, Clair, 48
Belichick, Bill, 14
Bilas, Jay, 3, 8
Bird, Larry, 6, 132
Blocked shots, 123, 126
Blocking out, 163–64
Blue-sky thinking, 74
Body measurements, 91–92
Boston Celtics, 31, 35
Box drill, 92–93
Bradley, Bill, 4, 31
Brady, Tom, 14
Brinkley, David, 57
Brooks, Herb, 12
Brown, Hubie, 22
Brown, Larry, 6, 19, 22
Bryant, Kobe, 5, 22
Bryant, Paul, 9
Buckley, Tim, 97
Buddy system, 105–6

Caldwell, Nikki, 149
Carlson, H. C., 83
Carnegie, Andrew, 45

Carnesecca, Lou, 94
Carril, Pete, 15
Carter, Vince, 5
Cartwright, Bill, 105
Chamberlain, Wilt, 71
Chaney, John, 147
Chapman, Joe, 28, 61, 88, 106, 113
Chicago Bulls, 13–14, 28, 71
Coaches
    advice for, 45
    characteristics of effective, 46–53
    ethics of, 51–52
Coaching profession, 54–55
Coaching Team Basketball
    audience for, 9–10
    purpose of, 10
Coach's Game Plan, 26, 36–39, 54–55, 72, 79, 97, 118, 150, 166
Code of Ethics for coaches, 51–52
Commitment, line of, 105
Communication, team
    eye contact, 112–13
    huddles, 114–16
    importance of, 112
    input, 116
    point to the passer, 113–14
    stand for a teammate, 114
Compassion, 50
Competitiveness, 50
Cords, Bill, 16, 17, 43
Core values
    defining, 59–66
    at forefront, 68
    game plan activities for, 72
    list of qualities and, 67
    selection of, 100
    team ownership of, 68–71
Coughlin, Artie, 122

Courage, personal, 47–48
Court sprint, 93
Covey, Stephen, 21, 73, 77
Crean, Tom, 32, 46, 48, 51, 58, 70, 95
Crum, Denny, 152

Daly, Chuck, 163
Dead ball situation, defending in, 157
Defense
    ATTACK acronym, 153
    blocking out, 163–64
    contesting a shot, 162
    essentials of, 153–54
    as heart of game, 151–52
    post defense, 160
    pressure on the ball, 156–57
    sprint back on defense, 154–55
    statistics, 165
    stopping dribble penetration, 159
    stopping pick-and-roll, 160–61
    summary of points on, 166
    talk on, 156
    unnecessary fouls, 164–65
Defensive rebounds, 123, 125
Deflections, 157–59
Deprey, Derek, 47
Diagrams, key to, xix
Diener, Travis, 16, 17, 18, 26, 27, 30, 34, 60, 63, 69, 70, 77, 78, 89, 108, 112
Disney, Walt, 76
Dribble penetration, 140–41, 150, 159
Driving line, 140
Dumars, Joe, 22
Dwyane Wade Legacy of Leadership Award, 102, 103

Emerson, Ralph Waldo, 46
Esprit de corps, 34–36
Ethics, Code of, 51–52
Explosive measurements, 93
Eye contact, 112–13

Fast-break basketball, 148
Ferry, Danny, 23
Field goal percentage, 123, 124, 126
Field goals attempted, 123, 124
Field goals made, 123–24
Fielitz, Dr. Lynn, 122
Fitzgerald, Dan, 86, 108
Fitzgerald, Jack, 109
Floor balance, 148–49
Foreign versus American players, 6–7
Fouls, personal
    defense and, 164–65
    as statistical factor, 123, 125, 126
Fraschilla, Fran, 5, 6, 50, 75
Free throw percentage, 123, 125
Free throws, 130–31
Free throws attempted, 123, 125
Free throws made, 123, 124, 126
Fry, Ed, 122

Gardner, Jack, 121–22
Grant, Horace, 14
Green, Kyle, 97
Green Bay Packers, 30
Grimm, Chris, 82, 83

Half-court offense, 179–85
Halftime lead, 123, 126
Hannum, Alex, 71
Harris, Del, 156
Haskins, Don, 151
Hayes, Woody, 53
Height, 91
Hill, Napoleon, 75
Holman, Nat, 82
Holsopple, Scott, 91, 111
Holtz, Lou, 50
Holzman, William, 156, 166
Horn, Darrin, 97
Howell, Bailey, 139
Huddles, 114–16

Important tasks, focus on, 50–51
Input, soliciting, 116, 118

Integrity, 46, 60, 83
Izzo, Tom, 96

Jackson, Marcus, 21, 64
Jackson, Phil, 13, 28, 71, 75, 108
Jackson, Robert, 78, 112
James, Dominic, 21, 22, 87, 110,
    114, 163
Johnson, Magic, 6, 87–88
Johnson, Ted, 69
Jones, Bobby, 114
Jones, Damon, 32
Jordan, Michael, 6, 7, 13, 14, 28, 71,
    188

Karl, George, 8
Kellaher, Barb, 106
Kerr, Steve, 28, 33
King, Martin Luther, 48, 76
King, William, 48
Kipling, Rudyard, 13
Knight, Bob, 48, 93, 139, 167
Kowalczyk, Tod, 96
Krause, Jerry, 153
Krzyzewski, Mike, 8, 28, 59, 112,
    114
Kuiper, Denny, 85

Laettner, Christian, 23
Leadership, shared, 102
Leg whip, 135
Live ball situation, defending in,
    156–57
Location of game, 123, 126
Lockwood, Dean, 149
Lombardi, Vince, 30
Lott, Jamil, 87
Louisiana Superdome, 77–78
Loyalty, 63–64

Marquette University. *See also*
    names of Marquette players
    basketball practice, 90
    core values of, 59–66
    esprit de corps, 35–36
    teamwork at, 16–18

Matthews, Wesley, 27, 87, 110
Maxwell, John, 43
McGuire, Al, 35, 36, 74, 129
McNeal, Jerel, 22, 87, 91, 110, 163
Mental toughness, 47–48
Merritt, Scott, 17, 112
Meyer, Don, 153
Meyer, Ray, 154
Miami Heat, 32, 187–89
Michaels, Al, 12
Mission Essential Task List, 50–51
Montgomery, Bernard, 53
Moore, Lt. Gen. Hal, 116, 117
Motor skills, 90–93
Mourning, Alonzo, 30, 187

Naismith, Dr. James, 3
NBA, influence of, 7–8
Nelson, Donnie, 7
Nessler, Brad, 66
New England Patriots, 14–15
Newell, Pete, 93
Nickel, Lori, 65
Novak, Steve, 20, 22, 28, 63, 78, 85,
    86, 87, 102, 112, 114

Offense
    dribble penetration, 140–41
    floor balance, 148–49
    free throws, 130–31
    offensive rebounding, 138–39
    outnumbering situations, 148
    passing ball inside, 131–38
    protecting the ball, 147
    receiving screens, 142
    screens-on-the-ball, 143–45
    seeing the floor, 139–40
    setting screens, 141–42
    shot selection, 146–47
    six goals, 149
    summary of points on, 150
    two most important factors,
        129–30
Offensive rebounds, 123, 125
Oliver, Richard, 15
Olympic Games, 5–6

O'Neal, Shaquille, 8, 22, 30, 187
Outnumbering situations, 148
Owens, Terrell, 15

Paint points, 131
Panaggio, Dan, 7, 20
Passion, 46–47
Paterno, Joe, 16
Patience, 71
Patton, George, 12
Paxson, Jim, 14
Payton, Gary, 8, 187
Peer coaching, 108
Peer pressure, positive, 69–70
Penetrate and dish, 141
Penetrate and kick, 141
Penetrate and score, 141
Personal fouls
    defense and, 164–65
    as statistical factor, 123, 125,
       126
Pick-and-pop, 145
Pick-and-roll, 144, 150
Pim, Ralph, 44, 49, 122
Pin and spin, 135
Pippen, Scottie, 14, 188
Player qualities, 26–30
Player selection
    character, 82–89
    list of requirements, 93–94
    motor skills, 90–93
    summary on, 96
    talent and dedication, 81–82
Player self-assessment, 37–39
Plays
    baseline out-of-bounds, 168–74
    half-court offense, 179–85
    sideline out-of-bounds, 175–78
    successful coaches and, 167
    summary of points on, 185
Posey, James, 188
Powell, Colin L., 19, 81, 95
Practice, watching, 90
Pressure on the ball, 156–57
Princeton players, 15–16

Qualities and values of teams, 67
Qualities of team player, 26–30

Rabedeaux, Jason, 45, 101
Ramsay, Jack, 11
Raymonds, Hank, 35
Recruitment of players
    character of player, 82–89
    as inexact science, 94
    input from team members, 102
    list of requirements, 93–94
    motor skills, 90–93
    summary on, 96
Respect, 60–61, 83–84
Responsibility, 62, 84–86
Riley, Pat, 19, 33, 57, 58, 69, 76, 187
Rivers, Glenn, 35, 104
Road rules, 100–101
Robertson, Oscar, 5, 26, 104
Role models
    Bill Russell, 4, 28, 31, 32, 35, 49
    Dwyane Wade, 9, 16, 17, 29, 30,
       31, 32–34, 69, 70, 78, 84,
       89, 91, 108, 109, 112, 131,
       188, 189
Roles, defining, 103–5
Rosniak, Todd, 90
Russell, Bill, 4, 28, 31, 32, 35, 49

Sampson, Kelvin, 7
Sanders, Terry, 112
Schwab, Trey, 78
Schwarzkopf, Norman, 12
Screen-on-the-ball, 143–45
Screens
    receiving, 142
    setting, 141–42
Seeing the floor, 139–40
Selection of players
    character, 82–89
    list of requirements, 93–94
    motor skills, 90–93
    summary on, 96
    talent and dedication, 81–82
Self-assessment, player, 37–39

Self-improvement, 53
Selfless service, 20–22
Shakespeare, William, 104
Sharman, Bill, 41, 119
Shot selection, 146–47
Shrink the circle, 106–7
Sideline out-of-bounds plays, 175–78
Slip, the, 145
Smith, Dean, 19, 25, 68, 111, 112, 113, 114
Snyder, Quin, 23
Soldier's Creed, 68
Speakers, outside, 116–17
Speed, 92
Spotlighting, 117
Sprint to the glass mentality, 138, 150
Standing reach, 92
Statistical factors
    conclusions on, 126
    research studies on, 122–23
    as scientific evidence, 121–22
    study results on, 123–26
    summary of points on, 127
Statistics
    defensive, 165
    offensive, 149
Steals, 123, 126
Summitt, Pat, 1, 26, 50, 132, 142, 149
Synergy, 21

Teaching teamwork, 19–20
TEAM (Together Everyone Achieves Miracles), 11
Team communication
    eye contact, 112–13
    huddles, 114–16
    importance of, 112
    input, 116, 118
    point to the passer, 113–14
    stand for a teammate, 114
Team ego theory, 4
Team play
    application model for, 9–10
    basketball's inventor and, 3

foreign players and, 6–7
NBA's influence on, 7–8
new generation and, 4–5
Olympic Games and, 5–6, 8–9
summary of points on, 10
Teamwork, examples of
    Chicago Bulls, 13–14, 28, 71
    Marquette University, 16–18
    New England Patriots, 14–15
    Princeton players, 15–16
    U.S. Hockey Team in 1980, 12
Tenacity, 64–66
Thompson, George, 26
Thompson, John, 5, 74
Three-point field goal percentage, 123, 124
Three-point field goals attempted, 123, 124
Three-point field goals made, 123, 124
Total rebounds, 123, 125, 126
Toughness, mental, 47–48
Townsend, Todd, 62, 78, 112
Transition defense, 154–55
Triple-threat position, 139, 140
Turnovers
    reducing, 147
    as statistical factor, 123, 125

U.S. Hockey Team in 1980, 12
U.S. Men's Basketball Team
    decline of, 5–6
    future of, 8–9
U.S. players versus foreign players, 6–7
Unselfishness, 62–63, 86–88

Value-based coaching, 53–54
Values, core
    activities, 72
    defining, 59–66
    at forefront, 68
    list of qualities and, 67
    selection of, 100
    team ownership of, 68–71

VanDerveer, Tara, 45
Vertical jump, standing, 93
Vision, shared, 75
Vision statement, 75–77, 80
Visual images, 77–79
Vitale, Dick, 140

Wade, Dwyane, 9, 16, 17, 29, 30, 31, 32–34, 69, 70, 78, 84, 89, 91, 108, 109, 112, 188, 189
Walker, Antoine, 187
Warlick, Holly, 149
Weight, 91
Weiss, Dick, 90
Westering, Frosty, 45
Williams, Pat, 74

WIN (What's Important Now), 50
Wingspan, 91–92
Winning plays
    baseline out-of-bounds plays, 168–74
    half-court offense, 179–85
    sideline out-of-bounds plays, 175–78
    successful coaches and, 167
    summary of points on, 185
Winter, Tex, 13, 35
Wooden, John, 6, 15, 22, 23, 47, 50, 91, 113, 142
Wootten, Morgan, 70

Zupanic, Tom, 79

About the Authors

Tom Crean has re-established Marquette men's basketball as one of the elite programs in the nation. In his six seasons, Crean has led Marquette to an average of more than 20 wins a year, won a conference championship, and made five post-season appearances, including the 2003 Final Four—the program's third appearance all-time and first since 1977.

Crean is a two-time recipient of the Ray Meyer Conference USA (2002, 2003), NABC District XI (2002, 2003), and USBWA District V Coach of the Year Awards (2002, 2003). He was named the 2003 Coach Clair Bee Award winner and a finalist for the 2003 Naismith National Coach of the Year Award. His 65.2 winning percentage and 122 victories rank third and fourth, respectively, all-time at Marquette.

Personally driven by an intense commitment to improve, Crean has structured a program at Marquette that focuses heavily on individual instruction. Through six seasons, Marquette players have earned 14 All-Conference selections. The program won its first conference player of the year award when Dwyane Wade earned Conference USA's top honor in 2003. Wade also went on to become the first Marquette player since 1978 to be named an Associated Press First Team All-American and finalist for the John R. Wooden Award. In 2005, Travis Diener joined Wade as players under Crean's mentoring who earned All-American and All-Conference honors, as well as going on to be selected in the NBA draft.

Crean's passion and commitment on the court has paid dividends off of it. The program has set total attendance records in each of the last three seasons and, since his arrival in 1999, has drawn more than 1.3 million fans.

Crean was named the 15th head coach in Marquette basketball history on March 30, 1999. Before arriving in Milwaukee, Crean served on the Michigan State basketball staff for four seasons, holding the position of associate head coach for the last two. During that time, the Spartans compiled an 88-41 record and made four consecutive post-season appearances, including a trip to the 1999 Final Four. As Michigan State's recruiting coordinator, Crean was instrumental in bringing two-time Big Ten Player of the Year Mateen Cleaves and 2000 John R. Wooden Award finalist Morris Peterson to East Lansing.

Prior to his tenure at Michigan State, Crean spent the 1994–95 season as an assistant coach at Pittsburgh and served as the associate head coach at Western Kentucky from 1990 to 1994. Crean got his start in coaching at the Division I level in 1989–90, serving on Jud Heathcote's staff at Michigan State.

A native of Mount Pleasant, Michigan, Crean earned his bachelor's degree in parks and recreation with a minor in psychology from Central Michigan in 1989. While pursuing his degree, Crean coached basketball at Alma College and Mount Pleasant High School.

Ralph Pim is an associate professor and chief of competitive sports in the Department of Physical Education at the United States Military Academy at West Point.

Prior to his arrival at West Point in 2000, Pim served as chairperson of the physical education department and head men's basketball coach at Limestone College in South Carolina. Pim coached basketball at the secondary and collegiate levels for 25 years. As a collegiate head coach, Pim built Alma College in Michigan and Limestone College into highly successful programs. His Alma teams were ranked nationally for points scored and three-point field goals, and the 1989 squad recorded the school's best overall record in 47 years. He also coached at Central Michigan, William and Mary, Northwestern Louisiana, and Barberton High School. Barberton won the 1976 Ohio State Championship and was selected the seventh best team in the country.

Pim spent 10 years as the technical advisor for the Basketball Association of Wales. He implemented training programs to facilitate the development of basketball throughout Wales, and he assisted with the training of their national teams.

Pim has authored six books on basketball and numerous coaching articles. He presented during the 2005 Naismith Basketball Hall of Fame Enshrinement Weekend and at the Final Four in 2004, 2005, and 2006.

A native of Akron, Ohio, Pim is a graduate of Springfield College in Massachusetts. He earned his master's degree from Ohio State University and his doctorate from Northwestern Louisiana State University. Pim is a member of the Phi Kappa Phi honor society. At West Point, Pim received the Brigadier General James L. Anderson Award for excellence in teaching in 2005. He also serves on the national committee for the Champions of Character for the National Association of Intercollegiate Athletics.